Have You Thought about Your Religion Lately?

HOLY
Hodgepodge!

Paul E. Sago

iUniverse, Inc.
Bloomington

iUniverse books may be ordered through booksellers or by contacting:

iUniverse
1663 Liberty Drive
Bloomington, IN 47403
www.iuniverse.com
1-800-Authors (1-800-288-4677)

ISBN: 978-1-4502-9752-3 (sc)
ISBN: 978-1-4502-9753-0 (hc)
ISBN: 978-1-4502-9754-7 (ebook)

Library of Congress Control Number: 2011903334

Printed in the United States of America

iUniverse rev. date: 03/08/2011

This book, along with my other accomplishments over the last twenty years, is largely the result of the love, encouragement, and daily assistance from my wife, Donna. She is my friend, advisor, and very special assistant in all things. I dedicate this book and my love to her.

Acknowledgments

My deep appreciation to Peggy Blackburn McCoy for encouragement during the writing process and her generous comments in the foreword.

Thanks to my good friends, Harvey and Wendy Holt, Linda Tomb, and Kevin Ogden for providing immeasurable assistance by proofreading early copy and suggesting improvements for my manuscript.

I appreciate the professionals at iUniverse who were so generous with their guidance and technical support during the publishing process. Special thanks to Kimberley West, my publishing consultant.

Special thanks to my wife, Donna, who did all the typing for the several preliminary copies and the final manuscript.

Contents

Foreword

Holy Hodgepodge is unique in its perspective and thought provoking in its content. The book does not provide answers so much as a clarifying pathway along which one is encouraged to think about his or her religion.

All my life I have tried to make sense of the concepts of God, love, sin, guilt, fear, and redemption. Somehow the pieces did not fit together. The whole thing was more like a jumble of jigsaw pieces that had been forced into ill-chosen spots.

Dr. Sago's book is refreshing in that he encourages readers to think for themselves. Each chapter is a wonderful "aha" experience.

If you ever wondered why, how, or if our lives relate to this awesome universe, then read this book.

If you are curious about life, religion, or our world, read this book.

If you wonder about or question the hows and whys of organized religion, read this book.

Be prepared to ponder, think, and consider your own philosophy of religion. It will be okay. The Creator of our universe can handle our questions.

Thank you, Dr. Sago, for giving your readers such a clear and simple, but oh so important, guidebook to help us be thinkers along the way.

One happy, thoughtful traveler,
Peggy Blackburn McCoy

Preface

During my preteen years, my closest friend lived just two blocks away. It was a small town. Everyone seemed to know everybody else's business (i.e., how they spent their time, when they got in at night, who various people were dating, and even the wrongdoing of some).

On the other hand, there were a few things that were personal, quiet, and unchanging. One of those was the father of my best friend. In public, he seemed to be congenial, happy, and easygoing. At home, he was a dictator. He was, in every way, the head of the house. On occasion, when I visited my friend, his father would make what seemed to be extreme demands on him. The father's opinion was—do it exactly this way and do it right now. If my friend dared to ask why, his father would say abruptly, "Because I said so; there need be no other reason!"

I considered that man to be harsh and insufficiently aware of the feelings of others. For a while, I thought that the father was the only person with such an attitude. Then I was introduced to the church. Believe it or not, in the church I found the same opinions held by my friend's rather caustic father. The attitude of organized religion seemed to be, "this is the way it is, because this is the way it has always been. It is written, it is doctrine, believe it, and ask no questions because we say so."

I am very inquisitive by nature. I need to know when, what, and why. I feel it necessary to investigate every possible avenue leading to a final opinion. Obviously, I am uncomfortable in the organized church. During my more than fifty years as a Christian college president, pastor, and counselor, I noticed that most people seemed to be satisfied with the church's answers to all questions. They sought no answers beyond doctrine. To me, such an attitude was—and is—unacceptable. So now, with all due respect, I write about it.

Introduction

It seems that many people, perhaps most, do not think seriously about their religion. Most folks, when shopping for an automobile, kick the tires, look it over carefully, and, in all probability, test drive different makes and models before making a purchase. When looking for a place to live, they examine the features of different houses or apartments; compare price, size, and location; and seriously discuss advantages and disadvantages of each property. Sometimes women shopping for shoes go to several stores and try on dozens of pairs before making a purchase. Those same people have, in all probability, accepted their religion without question.

Most young men and women of marriageable age, although looking forward to married life, would highly resent their family's involvement in an arranged marriage. However, when it comes to religion, beliefs are arranged. We simply borrow or accept in total what someone else tells us. It is customary—and generally expected—that we follow the same religious patterns and preferences as our parents and grandparents, even though the conditions surrounding us have significantly changed through the decades. The choice seems to be less thoughtful and more emotional.

Further, we tend to enthusiastically accept things said in church as absolute fact, even though we would question the same thought if it were expressed elsewhere. Our religion seems to work in a different emotional and logical realm than other areas of our lives.

I first started thinking seriously about this when I was a university president. I vividly remember a very bright senior coming to my office with a burning question a few weeks before graduation. She looked at me with total seriousness and said, "Dr. Sago, tell me how to be a godly person—and please leave out all the religious hodgepodge." I recall the feeling that came over me when I heard that question. I was astounded by my sudden realization of the enormity of "religious hodgepodge."

In the years since that conversation, I have been amazed at how often it has occurred to me that we claim our religion to be the most important thing in our lives—it determines not only the quality of life here, but also hereafter—yet we give it such little serious thought. We spend a lot of time with the hodgepodge.

This book is intended to be thought provoking, to entice you, the reader, to think seriously about your religious beliefs: what you really believe and why you believe it. It is not my purpose to be critical or to belittle any religious organization. Further, it is not my intent to change anyone's religious persuasion. However, I would have you think seriously about every detail of what you say you believe.

In some religions, thinking freely is not fully acceptable. Religious organizations tend to give answers long before the questions are asked. They tell you what to think, but not necessarily why, and the answers are usually not open for discussion. To question may be interpreted as doubt. To doubt would be sinful. Sinfulness leads to guilt. So why think? It seems much easier just to believe what you are told.

There is, I think, tremendous benefit in thoughtfulness—to dissecting religious positions, reconstructing them, bringing them up-to-date, and moving them from idealism to reality, from doctrinal statements to personal belief. Wonder has its rewards.

By writing this book, I hope to motivate the reader to think more seriously about what you have so easily, and sometimes rather casually, accepted as your belief about God and religion. I hope that the very process of thinking will bring forth a new and refreshing faith that will be more personal and meaningful.

Chapter I:

Borrowed Beliefs

I was born in the beautiful Ozark Mountains of southern Missouri during the third year of the greatest depression in the history of our nation. When I entered the world, Doctor Aubershon held me up by my feet and said to my father, "John, he has a head like a ten-cent watermelon!" Although my parents were not churchgoing people at that time, it was not many years until the religious notions of our little community filled my melon-like noggin.

By the time I was five, my folks were attending the First Methodist Church, which was just half a block from my grandpa Sago's general store and saloon. I had an interesting childhood listening to the hearty beer-drinking lead miners who filled the barstools at Grandpa's place through the week and then the influence of the Methodist Church on Sunday mornings. That particular Methodist Church was rather traditional; I don't think it could be classified as either liberal or conservative. There were usually no more than two or three kids my age in the Sunday school class and we were taught from five-by-seven-inch Sunday school cards with a picture on the front, a story of some sort, and a Bible verse to be memorized.

My religious orientation started early with those Bible verses, which I carefully set to memory. However, those early Biblical teachings were tempered a bit by the influence of the patrons at Grandpa's place. As I look back, the balance was not all bad.

As I grew into my teens, I attended the Church of the Nazarene on Sunday evenings and during spring and fall revivals. The Methodists did not have revivals, but the Nazarenes had evangelists two or more times a year for at least two weeks of rip-roaring revivals. The Church of the Nazarene was more fundamental in its approach to the scripture. However, it was not the Biblical teaching or the fundamentalist doctrine that drew me on Sunday night. It was the pretty girls who seemed to be abundant in the Nazarene congregation. One in particular was key to my regular attendance.

The Nazarene church building was originally built as a movie house, long and narrow. The youth sat at the very back of the sanctuary and were carefully watched by the more serious worshippers. One gentleman, I remember in particular, would kneel at the end of his pew during prayer, facing the back of the church, with the palm of his hand on his chin and his fingers spread wide over his eyes so that he could watch us closely. I guess you might say that he was keeping a watchful eye on the wayward. At that church, especially during revival time, I received much of my Biblical instruction, particularly about sin, God's judgment, and the wrath and damnation awaiting the unfaithful.

The third church in our little town was the Pentecostal Assembly of God. I seldom attended that church, but I did enjoy their annual fall brush arbor meeting in our town park. The brush arbor consisted of long poles draped across the top of already existing trees, with brush on top, creating a shelter from the evening dew. As an early adolescent, I was fascinated, sometimes a bit frightened, by the worshippers at the brush arbor events. At times, they would throw their heads back, shout praises toward heaven, and wave their hands in the air. Others would run up and down the aisles while praising God loudly. A few would actually roll on the ground during their fits of joyful worship. Those rustic and rambunctious brush arbor evangelistic services definitely influenced my religious beliefs.

As I look back, it is obvious that none of the folks in the churches in my small town were trained in Biblical studies or theology. Nevertheless, their convictions were firm and their Biblical interpretation was literal and without question. I am sure that I was heavily influenced by all three of those congregations—not only by the teachings of the ministers, but also by the daily lives of the town folk.

Many years have passed since those wonderful days in the Ozarks. I am now seventy-nine years old, and since those youthful days I have been to college, seminary, and graduate school. I have pastored four churches and acted as vice president or president of five universities, four of them church-related. However, after all the miles, the years, and the different experiences, reaching from Ohio to Southern California and back to the Midwest, I daily recall some experiences of those wonderful days in the Ozarks.

My small hometown in Missouri could have been considered the buckle of the Bible Belt. There may have been reason to doubt some of the theology there, but the spiritual fervor could never have been questioned. The saving of lost souls was preeminent, and "Oh, Why Not Tonight" was the favorite hymn for calling sinners into the Kingdom.

My first deep religious experience was when the fall revival was in full swing at the Nazarene Church. The guest preachers were two brothers from somewhere out in Kansas. They were both very talented, former nightclub entertainers—saved, sanctified, and set on a pathway of God's work as evangelists. I went to the revival every night. I was probably about twelve years of age. The revivalism got to me in a devastating way. Suddenly I was identified as a sinner, lost without hope. I was confused.

I will always remember one particular afternoon in late September during the fall revival time. I got my fishing pole, dug a can of worms, and headed for the pond about a mile and a half away. Getting to the fishing hole led me down through the lower end of town, across a vacant field, through Akers's barn lot and a wooded area. In that wooded area, on a large rock about the size and shape of a concert piano top, I stopped, sat down, and had my first serious conversation with God. Maybe it would be more correct to say the first time I talked seriously to God, because I don't remember any particular reply from Him. I asked God to help me understand what I had done to become so evil. I had tried to be good, I had never broken the law or been in jail, and the worst trouble I had experienced was the result of losing one of dad's tools or not finishing hilling the potatoes. But that was about it. At twelve, there had been no sex, alcohol, or girlie magazines, just an occasional glance at the ladies underwear section of the Sears Roebuck Catalog, which was in our outdoor privy for very practical purposes.

I sat on the rock for several hours. There were no sounds other than an occasional whippoorwill's song as afternoon began to turn into evening. I remember leaving the place, which I later referred to as "the rock," with an uncertain feeling. I had confessed all of my frustrations to God; I had asked Him to help me identify sins that may be in my life. Finally I promised, if He would guide me, I would live with the hope of pleasing Him.

I have often wondered if that experience on the rock was an adequate substitute for what the evangelist called "putting my all on the altar of sacrifice." It was hard because my all was not much. It was the Ozarks, during the Great Depression, and I was only a kid. Our lives back then were simple. There was not much to do that could be counted either good or bad.

To this day, I remember my experience at the rock. It gives me sort of a good, warm feeling just to think about it. I am not sure as to the extent of my forgiveness. I do not know if my sins were "washed away," but I do know that I felt better after that experience. It seemed that I became both more observant and receptive. My frustration level was much lower.

After the rock experience, I felt peaceful in church, even during the altar call. The call to sinners did not seem to include me, although I was not sure why that was so. I also became far more aware of the natural things in life: the clear flowing waters of the creek, the beautiful colors in the sunset, the radiance of a rainbow, and simple things such as the splash made by a jumping frog, or a bug crawling across the front porch. I seemed to be better connected to God and all of His creation. Fortunately, that connection has stayed with me through the years and I am very thankful.

When I think about God, who He is, and where He might be, my mind always goes back to that September experience on the rock.

It is a comfortable feeling that I am His, along with the bird that chirps, the frog that jumps, the bug that crawls, and the sun setting on a beautiful fall afternoon.

I have come to believe that my duty as the created may be very simply stated. That is, to love and honor the Creator and to love and protect the created all around me. Somewhere in all of these feelings of warmth, protection, and guidance, there is God. He is my God. I cannot give a physical description. He may not be physical at all. I cannot describe Him as a spirit because, as a human, I do not understand the spirit. But from the rock to this day, I am certain that God *is*.

I remember older people in my hometown, when explaining something rather difficult, would say, "Let me give you a 'fer instance.'" That is what I would like to do now.

At the time of my experience at the rock, I had no preconceived notions as to the image of God or the nature of God. My mind was open, something like a book with pages, but no print. The ministers at the Methodist and Nazarene Churches, to which I referred earlier, were good and honest men, but they were not theologians. Consequently, they had not confused me by painting mental pictures of God, although they referred to Him often.

When I went to the rock, I had no particular expectations. Since I had never been told that I should kneel when I prayed, I just sat there looking out over one of God's most beautiful handiworks and talked to Him as if He, too, were there. In my mind, I did not consider Him to be spirit or matter—just God. That is the way with youthful naiveté. Sometimes it is beneficial. I did not know if God would speak or if He would simply leave an impression. I did not know if I should go out and tell this story as a testimony, or keep it just between my God and me. I knew only one thing for sure: I felt better after talking to God—even though I did not know exactly who He was, where He was, or what He might want from me.

With all the unknowns—possibly what some would call complete ignorance of spiritual things, little guidance from the church, or any other religious influence—I walked away feeling something wonderful had been accomplished, although I didn't know just what it was. My life was definitely changed at the rock that day.

Perhaps the scriptures are correct when they speak about the necessity of becoming childlike. Children tend to be accepting, forgiving, and—above all—open to ideas and impressions. As we get older, we tend to become cautious, reserved, and sometimes hesitant to open ourselves to others or to God. Could it be the whole process has been unnecessarily complicated and that, in the end, it is just as easy as talking with a friend?

After my experience on the rock, I became more interested in the teachings of the Church and religious doctrine in general. In the following chapters, I discuss what I was taught and how I processed the doctrine through the years. As mentioned in the preface, it is my feeling that too many of us accept Christian doctrine without mentally processing and making it our own. It is important, I think, that our religion is truly ours—not borrowed.

Questions and Points to Ponder

- In their most formative years, most children only go to the church of their parents and grandparents. Would it be helpful to have children, especially in their intermediate years, experience several types of worship?

- How early in life should a child be told about God? How should the parent describe God? All too often, past methods have brought about fear.

- It is not necessary that every person have a religious experience such as "the rock." Is it necessary that we are able to look back at a specific time when we acknowledged God completely?

- Is it possible to simply "grow into" God, becoming spiritual in your outlook simply because of your environment?

- How much of your present religious beliefs are really yours—not borrowed?

Chapter II:

The Bible

In my hometown, the church's teachings from the Bible were set and rigid. I was taught that the Bible was absolutely God's Word. God had, Himself, written its pages or, in some cases, dictated directly to writers. His Word was not to be changed or questioned. Most of the churchgoers and local folks believed that the King James Version was the true and inspired Word.

Today, in many Christian churches, the clergy or worship leader, after reading the scripture in a church service or mass, follows by saying, "This is the Word of God for the people of God." The congregation then responds, "Thanks be to God." This may differ slightly according to denomination; however, the result is largely the same. It is impressed firmly upon the worshiper's mind—and, in most cases, quite conclusively—that this is the actual Word of God.

While waiting for a haircut at the barbershop in my hometown in Oklahoma, I overheard the barber say to the customer in the chair, "Have you heard any of that stuff about Mayan prophecy concerning the end of the world?" The customer replied, "No, I don't mess around with that kind of stuff. I accept the word of God directly out of the Bible. It's good for the end of time and everything else."

I can certainly understand people's acceptance of the Bible as the final answer to all questions. It's quick, easy, and convenient. Beyond that, we can interpret it to suit our particular notion about things.

On the other hand, perhaps we should occasionally rethink our position in the light of history and recent understanding. I often hear the word "retrofit." It is an interesting word meaning to add parts made available after the time of original manufacturing; in other words, to bring up to date by using all information or new creativity available. Perhaps there is such a thing as "retrofitting" our beliefs about the Bible and religion, such as adding all the information that has become available since its original writings.

As a kid, I enjoyed visiting my great-grandma Wallen. Her stuff and her routine intrigued me. My greatest fascination was her milk/cream separator. I loved dipping my finger into the sweet cream and tasting it just as her work was done. A close second was looking through Grandma Wallen's family Bible. I remember that it was big and had a hard cover like a textbook. On the front it said, "Holy Bible." I cannot recall reading a single word from that Bible, but I was impressed with its pages full of beautifully colored leaves, pressed flowers, family pictures, invitations to special events, obituaries cut from the newspaper, and an assortment of other family mementos. That was really my first introduction to the Bible—other than the memory verse cards from Sunday school. Not too impressive, I guess, from a theological standpoint. However, as I look back, my reaction was typical. I looked at her Bible not so much as an instrument to guide me in my life, but as a magical book. Its presence on the table seemed to be appropriate, necessary, and comforting.

As I grew older, I realized that many believers considered the Bible to be the authoritative word of God. Beyond that, they seem to view the Bible as a mystical, magical book—the very presence of which brings comfort. I have also observed that Bibles are displayed in most homes, but they seem to be largely a memento and untouched.

When I was a student pastor in northern Ohio, I drove out to the church area midweek to make calls on the parishioners. On one such occasion, there had been a death in a church family and the mother in the household where I visited was quite distressed. Noticing a Bible on her coffee table, I picked it up and read some of the promises of Jesus as recorded in the Gospel of John concerning the preparation of a place for us to go when we leave this world. She seemed to be comforted. Her six-year-old son was watching and listening with great interest. When I laid the book down, I said to her, "Thanks for the use of the Bible." Her son then said, "Mama saw you coming up the drive and told me to put it there. Most of the time we keep it in the closet on the shelf."

The Bible is one of the most popular books in history. The Good Book, as it is often known, has sold more copies than any other publication since the invention of printing. There are Bibles all over the world in hotel rooms, churches, synagogues, and in the majority of Catholic, Jewish, and Protestant homes.

In Judaism and Christianity, the Bible, at least the part appropriate to each religion, is considered to be the rule of law. However, of all the books ever written, the Bible is probably the most misinterpreted and misused. While its passages are quoted to bring benefit and comfort to hurting individuals and to give strength and hope in times of depression and despair, at the same time the Bible is used to promote guilt and bring notoriety and financial gain to selfish individuals.

The word "Bible" comes from the region of Byblos where the papyrus that was used in the production of the first scrolls, was grown. There is nothing magical or holy about the word *Bible.* Though it is often referred to as "The Book" or "The Good Book," the Bible, technically, is not a book, but a series of books. There are sixty-six books in all—thirty-nine in the Old Testament and twenty-seven in the New Testament. Some Bibles also have intertestamental books called the Apocrypha. The books of the Old Testament contain history, law, poetry, songs, prophecy and wisdom. The New Testament contains the Gospels (Matthew, Mark, Luke and John); letters written to various first-century churches, primarily by the Apostle Paul; letters to individuals; and the Book of the Revelation of John.

Technically, the Bible is not the word of God. It is a compilation of words that various people have written about God. Some Biblical scholars hold the view that the Bible was inspired by God (i.e., those who wrote were literally told what to say or write). The same scholars usually contend all that is written is totally correct and is, in fact, God's will. Other scholars state that it is the ideas and concepts—not the exact words—that were inspired. Still others, particularly those of the religious evangelical right, insist that God either wrote or directly dictated every word to the writers of the particular books within the Bible.

Think for a moment about the early education process for children. A child's earliest education is informal, but real and lasting. Parents say to toddlers, as they hold up a book, "book." This is repeated over and over. Logically, then, the child associates pages bound together with covers as a book. However, when a child reaches high school or college, he or she acknowledges that there are many books on hundreds of thousands of topics written in most of the world's languages. The word "book," then, raises many questions, the first being, "What book?" or "Why do I read this particular book?"

Sometimes a child is told to look up into the sky as his mother says, "bird," and then asks, "Jimmy, can you say *bird*?" The consequence is that forever in Jimmy's mind, everything that flies is a bird. However, Jimmy soon learns that there are many different types of birds. There are birds prominent in particular parts of the world, and not all birds fly.

However, when it comes to religion and the Bible, things are a bit different. A child is told as his father points to the Bible on the coffee table, "This is the Bible, the word of God." Usually, the child grows into adolescence, teen years, and adulthood and seldom questions whether that book is really the word of God or if God speaks in other ways.

When I was a small boy, I loved visiting Uncle Ben Robinson after coming home from school in the afternoon. Uncle Ben was not actually my uncle. Uncle was a term of endearment used for well-liked, kindly older men. I remember sitting on Uncle Ben Robinson's front porch. He would be in the rocking chair, telling me about boyhood experiences before there were cars, airplanes, or television. Uncle Ben was in the First World War. Sometimes he would tell me stories pertaining to those adventures. On one occasion, I told Uncle Ben that I was learning Bible verses as a project at the Methodist Church. I said that I could recite the Word of God. Uncle Ben listened and congratulated me upon the recitation. Then he said, "Sonny, you did good, but just remember, God ain't never written a book."

After considerable education in theology and Biblical studies, I have concluded that Uncle Ben was right; God does not write books. My personal belief is that God *does* send messages, and the sensitive, observant, and thoughtful person finds joy from them. For instance, for me, God writes indelibly in a Hawaiian sunset. One easily sees the mystery and the magnificence of God and creation in the face and well-formed fingers and toes of a newborn baby. Then consider the mountains, sculptured by the Great Artist of the universe. I agree completely with the writer of the eighth Psalm who said, "When I consider the heavens, the work of Thy fingers, the moon and the stars, which Thou hast ordained; what is man that Thou art mindful of him?" God has no need, after such wonderful things, to write words in Hebrew, Aramaic, Greek, or in any other language.

If God, with His own hand, did not pen the words of the Old or New Testament, where did all those stories come from? Biblical stories, particularly those of the Old Testament, were passed from generation to generation by oral tradition (i.e., told at family gatherings, on special days by fathers, and then repeated later by the sons, and finally by grandsons and future generations). The stories may have changed a bit in the telling and retelling over hundreds of years. However, I am satisfied that the messages remain true and may be as helpful today as in the time that they were first told.

It is sometimes troubling, though a bit amusing, to hear ministers and television evangelists make strong claims about God speaking to them just prior to their message, suggesting that God gave them the exact, much-needed words for those watching and listening. It is also interesting that, for the most part, those who claim to hear God's voice in an audible way usually hear him talk about matters that are their own pet peeves—subjects of social debate, political interest, or financing for their religious projects.

It does not diminish the power of the Bible for us to understand that it was written about God by men, some being uneducated and untrained, and that the writings came after generations of oral history. Those who wrote were good men who, for the most part, scribed what they had heard and what they had felt or experienced personally. Then, of course, scribes who were rewriting or readying for print those inspired words often, I believe, slipped in their own religious, social and personal biases—and sometimes may have changed things a bit as the result of instruction from church leaders. So, the Bible has good messages for the people who read and obey. If it is understood in context—and if small phrases are not lifted for ego boost under the pretense that they are exact directives for our journey—we may all benefit from Biblical studies.

Questions and Points to Ponder

- How old should a child be before receiving teaching about the Bible, particularly if those teachings are given as absolutes?

- Do parents have an obligation to explain to their children that the Bible was written about God, but not by God?

- Should we make great distinctions between the various versions of the Bible (i.e., King James, American Standard Version, New Modern Translation, etc.)—or should the differences be seen as retrofitting?

- Should it trouble you to consider that the Old Testament was written by Hebrews for Hebrews, largely to maintain their laws and culture?

- Do you find it difficult to acknowledge that the New Testament books were chosen from hundreds of manuscripts that were written primarily about the life of Christ and others by individuals who explained the meaning of Christ's message to the world?

Chapter III:

Mythology and the Bible

In my hometown, folks not only believed in the Bible, they carried the Bible with them often, particularly to church, funerals, or other religious gatherings. Most of the Bibles in those days were large and black, containing both the Old and New Testament. This was long before the days of paperbacks and variously colored Good Books. Nevertheless, whatever the size and color, for most people, that Book contained all the answers they needed to solve life's problems. I doubt if any of those good folks in my neighborhood would have agreed with the following thoughts pertaining to the Bible and mythology.

Folk stories, sometimes called myths, are interesting, and continue through generations by the telling and retelling. Consider the story of George Washington throwing a silver dollar across the Potomac. That's mythology, but there are several ways to react to that particular myth.

- Maybe he did, and maybe he didn't.

- Why would he want to do it?

- Did the dollar go all the way across the river?

- Did anyone ever find it?

- He must have had money to throw away.

- A dollar doesn't go that far today.

We could go on and on, embellishing such a folktale. But why? It was probably told to emphasize the strength of George Washington as a great man, one of our earliest leaders and first president. Whether he did or didn't throw a dollar across the Potomac or any other body of water makes little difference. The story probably did not change his life and certainly does not affect ours in any fashion other than curiosity. Such a story is called folklore or folk mythology.

Biblical mythology is quite different. From our early childhood, most of us have been taught that the stories in the Bible are true. Even as we grew to adulthood, few of us dared to ask whether certain Biblical stories were true or just folklore of the Hebrew people.

The story of creation in Genesis is classical Biblical mythology. The most troubling part of the creation myth, and Adam and Eve's exile from the Garden due to their disobedience, is the doctrine of original sin. Many religious organizations, both Protestant and Catholic, contend that because Adam and Eve sinned against God, their sin is inherited by us today. Therefore, we are all born with sin. Some churches baptize infants early to wash away that sin. Other churches wait until later and teach children of a responsible age that Christ came to die for their sins and if they accept his sacrifice, both inherited and committed sins will be forgiven.

Jewish rabbis took advantage of the theory of original sin. They taught all the Jewish people that they must sacrifice animals or birds and bring gifts to the temple so that their sins would be forgiven. Regularly there were required sacrifices of a calf or pair of doves, etc., depending upon the depth of their guilt. This practice continued for many years. Some writers prophesied that someday God, Himself, would find a way to set things right by removing the guilt of original sin. Consequently, the theory of Christ's sacrifice as a redemption for all time came into being as a final solution for sin.

The theory of original sin, which brought great profit to the Jewish priesthood, was further complicated by another myth of the Old Testament. God became displeased with all humanity. They were evil and sinful because of inherited and committed sin, so God decided to destroy the world and all its people with a great flood.

As God looked at humanity, there was one man and his family "who found grace in the eyes of the Lord." His name was Noah. God told Noah to build a boat large enough to hold all of his family and two of every kind of animal on the face of the earth.

Following God's instructions, Noah built the boat. Obviously, it was necessarily as large as our current day ocean liners since there were literally thousands of varieties of animals and birds and other creatures to be saved. (Its actual size is given in the Old Testament.) I can imagine Noah worked frantically. I can't decide where all the wood came from, how he could build a boat so large, or what the neighbors thought about this madman building such a vessel in the village square.

As the story goes, Noah finished the boat. He loaded it with his family and all the animals. Then he closed the door. What a stench there must have been! I hope the family lived topside!

After everything was loaded into the boat, it began to rain, and it rained forty days and forty nights until all the world was underwater. Of course, people writing the story thought the world was flat, so perhaps that seemed logical. But, given the fact that the world is round, a flood of that magnitude seems improbable. After forty days the rain stopped, and Noah sent out a dove. It flew around and finally came back with a leaf in its mouth, indicating that either there was a dry spot somewhere or the dove had picked up a floating leaf. Nevertheless, as the story goes, the water receded and everything started again. Adam's entire race was drowned, so from now on it was Noah's race. All those who had been condemned to original sin were dead. Therefore, isn't it logical to think that original sin would also be dead? Somehow the writers of the Old Testament skipped that part and carried original sin straight on through.

So everything was destroyed except Noah, his family, animals, birds, and original sin. That's the story. Although it was written by an Old Testament writer, I have always assumed his name was Ripley!

Now, let's move to the New Testament. Remember that original sin is still in play, and sacrifices are a necessity of life in the Jewish community. The synagogues and the priests prospered, but most of the people were poor. Some lived in adobe-type buildings in small villages. Others were itinerant farmers and sheepherders. The people continued to struggle, barely eking out food for their families, but always making their sacrifices in the temple and paying 10 percent of their income to the rabbis.

Then, according to the gospels in the New Testament, a male child was born to a couple from Nazareth. That child changed history. Joseph and Mary never had a sexual encounter, but somehow she became impregnated. As the story goes, she was visited by an angel and told of the impending pregnancy and delivery of a son who would be the savior of the world.

While Joseph and Mary were traveling to Bethlehem to pay their taxes, the child, Jesus, was born. A star began to shine over the place of his birth, and wise, wealthy astrologers from an eastern country came thousands of miles on speedy camels to worship him. The new baby drew so much attention that the king of the land wanted to meet him and probably dispose of him as an opposing force. Mary and Joseph took him to Egypt for safety. After things quieted down, they brought Jesus back to Nazareth and apparently he lived a rather quiet and normal childhood.

About age thirty, Jesus began to recruit some disciples and go around the countryside teaching that He was the Son of God, that He and the Father were one. He told his listeners, "If you have seen Me, you have seen the Father." Jesus convinced many of the people in and around Jerusalem that it was impossible to have fellowship with God or to worship God without going through Him.

Jesus's teachings upset the rabbis and other Jewish leaders. He ridiculed their sacrifices. He called for a new day in religion. The Jews saw Him as an opposing force, a radical revolutionary. So they put Him on trial and killed Him—death by hanging on a cross. Jesus was buried, and after three days, He appeared to his disciples alive. He talked about going away to a place where His followers could not go now, but would later be invited to come.

Then one day, he walked to the top of a mountain and disappeared into the clouds. Through all of this, eventually came one of the greatest religious movements in history—Christianity, to follow Christ.

After Christianity spread to Rome and was promoted by St. Augustine, Christian mythology became predominant in the empire. Later, the theology was carried north by Charlemagne and Christian theology began to be a part of European mythology. Germanic and Celtic mythology that was native to Northern Europe was pushed aside while Mary stories, Crusade myths, and myths about various saints took their place. The pre-Christian stories never completely left society and they eventually mingled with Roman Catholic frameworks to form new stories. The legend of King Arthur and his quest for the Holy Grail is an example of such new stories. There seemed to be two great opposing forces in Northern Europe: paganism and Christianity. At times when Christianity was popular, pagan myths were Christianized. At other times, Bible stories and Christian saints seemed to be of less interest to the population.

Since the end of the eighteenth century, Biblical mythology seems to have lost some of its previous excitement. Some Westerners no longer claim Christianity as their own mythological framework. Other scholars tend to believe that spiritualism is actually in our psyche and influences our ideals, such as the Christian idea of afterlife and heaven. Some groups in Western society are still strong on Christian mythology. It is their rule of life. But the idea that Christendom rules all aspects of society no longer seems applicable in our Western culture, particularly in the United States.

Some doubts were advanced because the writers of the New Testament, and apparently Jesus Himself, announced that certain events pertaining to the end of the world, the Apocalypse and His return, would be experienced in the lifetime of the people listening to His message. It didn't happen!

All the while, because of the guilt of sin, the Jewish people continued to make sacrifices to God, slaughtering animals, and killing doves, and destroying God's creation in an attempt to please Him. So, after centuries of sacrificing through the Judaic system, people heard about a new and miraculous way, an ultimate sacrifice for sin.

The idea of sin and sacrifice, particularly that of a one-time sacrifice by Christ to end the plague of inherited sin, is quite a relief to the human mind. The very thought that guilt can be removed by accepting Christ's great sacrifice is quite appealing. However, if the original event that resulted in inherited sin is a myth, then it stands to reason that the sacrifice or the consequence would also be extended mythology.

I have great respect for Christ as a leader of the apocalyptic movement and as a wise prophet and a charismatic leader. However, logic and reason, based on cause and consequence, does not support the redemption theory.

Prior to Christ's birth, there had been many reports of leaders with miraculous births. Kings, particularly those of Egypt, were believed to have descended from the heavens. Somehow the story of Christ's miraculous birth, death, and resurrection was taken more seriously and within three hundred years of his death, a major part of the Roman Empire had been, in some way, affected by His teachings and that of His followers, particularly a man named Paul, an itinerant preacher who wrote letters concerning his beliefs. Those letters eventually became a major part of the New Testament.

Today, the Bible remains the rule of life for many believers. Churches teach that believing makes it so. Nevertheless, there is a growing number of people willing to think seriously about what they say they believe.

Questions and Points to Ponder

- Do you find it troublesome to recognize that parts of the Bible are folklore?

- The Jewish rabbis were entrepreneurs. They used sin to solicit sacrifices, largely gifts to them.

- Some religious teachers and preachers today, especially some rowdy TV evangelists, play the sin card for all its worth.

- Would it shake your faith not to believe Mary was a virgin as we interpret virginity today—having never had a sexual encounter?

- Would there be fewer churches and less religious "hodgepodge" if we all worshipped God as the only Deity?

Chapter IV:

Creation

Throughout my childhood and teenage years, I was taught that the book of Genesis, particularly chapters one and two, was absolute fact. In the beginning, God created everything from nothing. He created the world, light and darkness, land and water, trees and shrubs, and all the animals and birds in five days. On the sixth day, he created man from the dust of the earth. He called the man Adam. Adam was to enjoy all that God had created.

Adam was lonely, so God put him to sleep, took out one of his ribs, and with it created a woman, Eve, to be his wife. On the seventh day, God rested. Because God rested on the Sabbath after a busy week, we should too.

Later, God placed Adam and Eve in the beautiful Garden of Eden, with one restriction: a certain tree in the garden should not be touched. Adam and Eve became curious and ate the fruit of that untouchable tree after Eve was tempted by a walking, Hebrew-speaking snake. As the result of their disobedience, God kicked them out of the garden forever with penalties: the woman would bear children in great pain, and the man would earn his living by the sweat of his brow. Even more serious, now they must face death. Adam and Eve blamed a snake, the devil.

As a young person, I often wondered what would have happened had Adam and Eve not sinned. Would they have lived forever, by themselves, in the Garden? Would Adam never have worked? Would

Eve have never borne children? If so, none of us would be around to know about creation. Also, it seems to me that even the most beautiful garden would become boring after a while if there was nothing to do: no work, no sex, just looking at the flowers. Beyond that, what about allergies? Wow! Those thoughts, and many others, I kept just between God and me. God never offered an explanation.

Now, in my later years, I still wonder. Where did everything come from: rivers, mountains, stones, trees, animals, or us? For everything, there is a beginning. There is movement and motion. Everything comes from someplace and is going somewhere. Where did we come from and where are we going?

Should we believe in creation or in evolution? Is there a third choice—one that is more probable?

Organized religion, particularly Protestantism and Catholicism, tends to accept the Jewish position as an absolute answer regarding creation. But how do we really know? What has fashioned our belief regarding creation? For most, our belief about creation is based on the story in Genesis and what we have been told to believe.

It could be that Genesis 1 was never intended to be history; maybe it was just a story to explain the unknown. It could have come about something like this: One day an inquisitive, young Jewish lad went to the rabbi with a question. After all, the rabbis were God's representatives; they had the final answer for all questions. "Teacher," he asked, "where did we come from? How did this world begin?" The rabbi's response may have been similar to that recorded in the first two chapters of Genesis. "One day, God decided that He would create a world. Perhaps He was tired of continually being with nothing: nothing to see, nothing to do, absolute nothingness."

According to Biblical theory, there was nothing to work with because nothing existed but God. That concept, in itself, is difficult. Think about it. No air, no clouds, no seas, no mountains, no stars, no day or night—absolutely nothing. It is no wonder that God wanted there to be something.

The Rabbi continued. After deciding to create a world, God considered the amount of time for such a vast undertaking. The very thought is perplexing, for if there was nothing, there was obviously no time. Somehow God started with nothing and created the whole world in six days. He first created a rather formless mass. Everything was dark. So he created light and then separated light from darkness. Next, God created and separated land from water and the earth from the heavens. The result was all the basic stuff: land, water, and air. Then it was time for trees and plants, birds and animals, and creatures of the sea. Finally, on the last day of work, God looked at what he had created. There was a lot of stuff, but no management. So God created man and woman to manage His creation. By the sixth evening, He was done. It was quite a week's work, even for God.

Thus, in the first chapter of Genesis, there are a lot of answers to a multitude of questions (e.g., where everything came from, the origin of the first six-day workweek, and the Sabbath as the day of rest). Many Christians accept the stories just as they are. They do not choose to be troubled by thoughtfulness.

Let's consider a different possibility for the beginning and formation process—a combination of creation and evolution. The word evolution means "a process of continuous change from a lower to a higher and more complex state; a theory that the various types of animals and plants have their origin in other pre-existing types and that the distinguishable differences are due to modification in successive generations; a process in which the whole universe is a progression of inter-related phenomena" (*Webster's Ninth New College Collegiate Dictionary*).

Most scientists agree that the earth started as a mass of molten, lava-like rock. Then with heating, cooling, expansion, retraction, and the addition of moisture, the rock hardened and stratified, and land formations protruded from the water. Additionally, it is assumed that the various continents have changed substantially over time. Perhaps Africa and South America were joined at one time—as were other landmasses. The part of the earth that now constitutes the United States and Canada was connected to other landmasses and was, according to geologists, partially south of the equator. New York is believed to have been in the southern hemisphere.

Evolution suggests continuous change over millions—perhaps billions—of years during which, in some way, amoebas became animals and/or paramecia became people.

Obviously, the earth as we know it today has not always been present. The world we inhabit has been transformed many times since the hard rocky thrust of continents and the gigantic oceans first formed billions of years ago. We—and the world around us—have grown through the ages, most recently the Stone Age, the Bronze Age, the Iron Age, the Industrial Period, and the Nuclear Age.

Scientists, through carbon dating and other methods, have determined that the earth is billions of years old. Two and a half billion years ago, in the Paleozoic Era, the age of marine invertebrates began. Then in the Mesozoic Era, from 345 million years to 190 million years ago, there was the growth of forest, the first dinosaurs, flying reptiles, and flowering plants. Beginning 65 million years ago, during the Cenozoic Era, came primates, modern mammals, grasslands, the uplifting of mountains, and humans. I can easily believe that God did it. He may have done it over billions of years. It may have been somewhat less. However God did it, it is wonderful and mindboggling.

People who interpret the Bible literally choose to believe that on the sixth day God created Adam and Eve from the dust of the earth. No other living beings—other than those created during the previous five days—enjoyed life upon the earth. Yet there seems to be sufficient evidence of Neanderthal and other intermediate stages of human beings, some who walked on all fours until emergence of the *Pithecanthropus Erectus*. There is evidence, not only from study of the world formation, but also from hieroglyphics and drawings on cave walls, ancient tools, etc., that human beings evolved as a species.

There is substantial evidence supporting evolution as a combination of divine creativity and a natural physical evolving. Consider pregnancy, which results in birth. Of all the wonders of creation, birth may be the most wonderful of all. The process starts when a microscopic sperm from a male joins an equally small, single-celled egg in the woman and a multiplication of cells begins creating the development of organs and form. Nine months later, what was just a union of egg and sperm becomes a living, human being. The little person enters the world with sight and hearing, with fingers and feet that grasp and move. For months, the new human being cannot stand or walk. The baby crawls. Then, in time, the process continues, and the baby not only stands, but walks and later talks. Then fortunately, or unfortunately as may be your experience, this new and innocent formation becomes an adult. The process of evolution is continuing. The body grows and strengthens through maturity and then begins to deteriorate in strength and mass, always moving toward something.

The purpose at this point is not to give a detailed or scientifically correct analysis of the development of the earth or mankind, but rather to recognize that the evolutionary process is reasonable and possible. There seems to also be evidence that the evolutionary process is continuing. As an example, think about athletes—particularly basketball players—of sixty years ago. Most high school senior athletes were less than six feet in height. Occasionally, there was a seven-foot-tall athlete. Such giants were acclaimed across the country. Now, in the twenty-first century, a six-foot-tall athlete in the NBA is considered short, and to be seven foot or taller is commonplace.

So is the answer creation or evolution? While the Biblical literalist may object to the very thought processes suggested here and maintain that the faithful should stand firmly on the Genesis account, it seems reasonable to believe that we are not forced to choose precisely between creationism and evolution. Perhaps the answer is Creative and Controlled Evolution.

Let us assume that there is a Divine Architect—a Creator and Coordinator of the universe. Perhaps it is sufficient to acknowledge that our universe is complex, and that we understand only a small fraction of its magnitude. Could it be that a creative and spiritual Guide of the universe has always been and still is in charge? Creation may have been as brief as a week or required billions of years; in either case, time does not limit the wonder and majesty of the universe or the spiritual force that prompted and guides its courses.

So, what shall we say about Creative Evolution? Who did it? Is it finished? Are we still evolving? I believe firmly that the Divine Creator guided the formation of the universe over millions of years and that evolution is still happening today. Therefore, our final being and our final destination are unknown.

I usually carry a small rock from my collection. The stone I have carried for the last several months came from the Big Island of Hawaii. It is volcanic lava, mixed with other earth forms as it flowed from deep within the earth, and somehow ended up in the beautiful waters of the Pacific. That is where I found it. Now, as I hold it, I am reminded of the awesomeness of the Creator, the wonders of creation, the vastness of time, all unfathomable. Most of all, it tells me that—although I cannot define Him—God is and I am. However, what I am, compared to God and his total creation is minute—like a bug on the windshield of time.

Questions and Points to Ponder

- Do you find it troubling to acknowledge that the world existed millions of years before the Genesis story of creation?

- Does it diminish God or your own spirituality to acknowledge that creation has been in process for millions of years and is continuing today?

- Have you ever noticed the layers of rock in mountains that suggest eons of time?

- Humans may not have come directly from another form of animal; however, it seems reasonable that our species has evolved over many centuries and is still evolving.

- Are you able to mentally process creative and controlled evolution as opposed to instantaneous creation?

Chapter V:

Sin

The several churches that I attended during my youth differed somewhat in doctrine. However, they agreed on one basic belief that I have never understood. I still struggle with that belief today. It seems to be too petty and mean-spirited to be associated with God. That teaching is the doctrine of original sin. The Jewish rabbis taught it and now most Protestant and Catholic churches teach that because Adam and Eve disobeyed God, their sin somehow was extended to us and becomes an inherited curse. I am a sinner and you are a sinner because Adam sinned. How could that be? People are born *with* sin just because two people, according to the story in Genesis, chose to disobey God thousands of years ago?

The doctrine of original sin could only be concocted in the human mind. It is far too vengeful to be divine. The doctrine is childish. Think of it as a group of children playing. They are all friends and live in the same general area. One of the children becomes angry; he yells out at the others saying, "I don't like you and I don't like your parents. I don't like the rest of your family who are not even born yet." Now that is childish! However, there is a bright side. Within minutes, children forgive and forget and start playing again; but the childish story of Adam and Eve's sin goes on and on.

Before delving into the topic of original sin—sometimes referred to as inherited sin—it is necessary, again, to give serious thought to the creation story in Genesis. Adam's sin was the result of disobedience to God's instruction (i.e., both he and his wife, Eve, chose to eat of the forbidden fruit after being tempted by the devil). That defiance was the first sin and is now referred to as original sin. The believers in original sin contend that the sin of Adam and Eve and the sinful nature of all men thereafter, is the result of that disobedience.

The Apostle Paul refers to that doctrine in his letter to the Romans, chapter 5, verse 12: "Through one man sin entered into the world, and death through sin, and so death spread to all men."

Let us think logically for a moment. Adam and Eve sinned. The result: sin became an inheritance of all humans who followed them. So we have a case of incident and consequence (i.e., Adam's sin and inherited sin). It follows logically that without the incident, there would have been no consequence. The most widely accepted definition of the word *consequence* is the effect, result, or outcome of something occurring earlier. Assuming the Garden of Eden story, along with the creation of man, is a myth—just a story to illustrate a point or explain the unknown—then the consequence would also be mythology. Therefore, with no original sin, there could not—and would not—be inherited sin. Let's consider several factors that relate to this conclusion.

The Genesis story states that the creation of Adam and Eve was the origination of humanity—all other humans are descendants from them. It is also stated that their creation was on the sixth day. Although the creation story emphasizes day-by-day progression, most Biblical scholars contend that the six days of creation are metaphoric, particularly those days before the creation of a sun and moon.

Another consideration involves the date of the creation of man, according to Genesis. Biblical scholars have, for many years, attempted to calculate the exact date of creation. Those dates range from the earliest of 5501 BC by J. Africanus to the most recent of 3836 BC by A. Helwigius. The better-known Ussher dating of creation is 4004 BC (Floyd Nolen Jones, *The Chronology of the Old Testament*, 16th ed.).

The above dates are very important in our consideration because most anthropologists and primatologists agree that "modern man," who well represents humanity of today, evolved in Africa 200,000 years ago. They migrated from Africa into what is now Central Europe between 70,000 and 50,000 years ago. Obviously, the earth was formed billions of years previously, and the age of dinosaurs, which has been of so much interest to our youth in recent years, was during the Jurassic Period, some 190 million years ago.

In July 2010, *National Geographic* reported that a skull of a woman, estimated to be four million years old, recently had been found in Ethiopia. If we accept the findings of science, substantiated well by the discovery of early human remains, DNA extractions, primitive tools, and carbon dating, we must conclude that the Biblical creation story is mythological. As pointed out in an earlier chapter, such a conclusion does not necessarily eliminate God's hand in creative evolution.

Admittedly, it is not possible for humans to understand God's intent. We can only think about it in relationship to what we consider to be the nature of God (i.e., loving, kind, long-suffering, forgiving, and redeeming).

Thoughtful readers of the Bible have some difficulty comparing God as the Father in the prodigal son story with the God who so quickly kicked Adam and Eve out of the garden. Then, rather than forgiving or giving his creation a second chance, He condemned them to a more difficult life and impending death. If the Genesis story is considered to be true regarding creation and the initiation of sin, we are caused to wonder about God's intent. Why would God create Adam and Eve, place them in a garden with instructions "not to touch anything" if, as we have always been told, He knew their actions even before they acted?

Think about a toddler walking in a stumbling manner around the living room, holding on to chairs, and wobbling to the coffee table. On the coffee table is a precious and fragile family heirloom. Mommy and Daddy yell in unison, "Jimmy, don't touch!"

We have all experienced something like this incident. Obviously when little Jimmy is told, "Don't touch," it seems "don't" is unheard or dismissed. Touching that item becomes the central theme on little Jimmy's mind. It would seem simpler and more convenient for the parents, and much better for Jimmy's psyche, if they simply moved the precious item to a safer place until Jimmy was old enough to understand its value.

It is difficult for me to believe that shortly after creating them, God positioned Adam and Eve for certain failure. Obviously, "Don't touch that tree," did not work and, of course, God knew it wouldn't. Such action does not seem consistent at all with my understanding of the loving and forgiving nature of God.

In my counseling sessions over the last fifty years, many people have acknowledged their frustration as children when they were told about their inheritance of sin. Such an accusation seems not only shocking to a child, but is, in all probability, damaging to his sense of self-worth. They feel flawed! Perhaps they are shocked even to the extent they are thinking, "I am already stained with sin having done nothing to deserve it, why not just live it up!"

Thinking back to my experience at the rock, there were two burning questions in my mind: What have I done to cause this sin, and can I be forgiven for sins of which I am unaware? I, like others, was told that if we confess, God will forgive us. If we cannot identify our sins, how do we know what to confess? Certainly, the idea of inherited sin has damaged generations of people who deserved a better way.

Perhaps there is a better way. Consider this: instead of telling our children that they are born into and with sin, tell them that they are born pure and clean and loved by God. Then, instead of living life as sinners attempting to become clean, they could start life pure with the goal of staying as clean as humanly possible. The psychology of such teaching would seem to be completely in our favor and an honor to our Creator.

Obviously, in the process of living, we do sin against our Maker, sometimes intentionally, and sometimes unknowingly. Something as simple as not honoring His creation is, I think, a sin against God. Certainly those of us who have lived in this last generation have played havoc with our wonderful world and, at times, with each other. Surely, such behavior does not honor God.

Sin is generally understood to be the transgression of divine law or the willful violation of religious or moral principles. Sins have traditionally been divided into two categories: mortal sins, which destroy our lives and set us on the path to eternal damnation; and venial sins, which are, by comparison, relatively minor. In spite of these definitions, some churches hold to the position that sin is sin! Any unforgiven sin puts our spiritual lives in jeopardy.

The whole idea of sin seems to differ with geographic location, financial levels, social standing, and church denominations. In some religious circles, social drinking is well accepted; in other more fundamental groups, alcohol is strictly forbidden. At one time, ministers spent a great deal of their energy preaching about women's clothing. The depth of her religious commitment seemed to depend on the length of her dress. Some denominations preached against cosmetics; others held that any adornment—necklaces, bracelets, earrings, even wedding rings—were inappropriate. One of my pastors was among the negative who felt women should be plain and appropriate in their dress. However, in his later years, he confided to me that he thought that maybe a little paint would help any old barn. That comment was his way of using humor to admit that his attitude had been a bit extreme all along.

I remember ministers preaching against dancing when I was a boy. At age thirteen, I was a Boy Scout in the Frankclay, Missouri, troop. Much to our pleasure, Boy Scott meetings and Girl Scout meetings were held on the same night at the high school. The Girl Scout leader and our Boy Scout master decided that some training in social dancing would be a contribution to our maturity and prepare us as we approached the Junior-Senior Prom time. Of course, the Boy Scouts in particular were delighted, and we immediately thought about which Girl Scout we most wanted as a dance partner. The plan went along magnificently. It was fun—and definitely improved our social graces. Everything was going along well. A girl named Wanda was my dance partner and I looked forward to every Boy Scout meeting, even to the extent of dabbing on a bit of my dad's aftershave before heading toward the high school.

Then it all ended abruptly. Some of the town's busybodies reported our dancing to the Nazarene pastor. He, along with the hesitant support of the Methodist pastor, appeared at our next meeting. We could all hear them in the hall talking with the scout leaders in excited tones. That was the end of our dancing. It had become a religious issue.

After the sudden halt of our dance times at the high school, I did not find other ways or means to continue dancing. Consequently, as an adult, I did not dance. My wife was also raised in a fundamentalist environment and had never learned to dance. When we moved to a new university assignment in California, our first social function was the Annual Alumni Valentine Dance. There we sat, the university president and his wife, neither knowing how to dance. It was, to say the least, uncomfortable. Not that my wife or I were troubled with any sinfulness related to dancing, but we found it a bit difficult to explain to our friends why we did not dance without going into religious matters. The alumni and their spouses had a great time, but for the most part, we missed it. The next morning, Donna and I decided to sign up for dance lessons at Arthur Murray. We attended weekly lessons for two years and found dancing to be very wholesome, relaxing, and a bonding activity for us. Since that time, we are both enthusiastic about ballroom dancing.

The Bible makes few references to dancing. One that always interested me was in II Samuel 6:14. David, in his enthusiasm over the Ark of the Covenant coming into town, danced in the streets, partially clad. I can't imagine myself going to that extent, but generally speaking, dancing seems to me to be a wholesome and fun activity.

As I have become older, I am of the opinion that sinning is a very personal matter (i.e., sin can be a matter of thought or action). Further, I feel that what may be sin for one person, may not necessarily be sin for another. If I consider something to be sin and do it anyway, for me it would be sin or at least depressing. That same act may not be spiritually troubling to others. It is quite convenient for any one of us to point out the sins of others. The less wealthy may point out the sinfulness of the rich. The strict fundamentalist may speak in a nitpicking manner about a Christian neighbor because of minute doctrinal differences. Of course it is easy for the petite to point out the sin of gluttony, or for the obese to criticize a friend for taking undue pride in their exercise regimen. I have learned, after all these years, that living a life of kindness is a full time job. Certainly, I do not have time or reason to criticize others about spiritual matters. It is quite possible, I think, that God may be happy with me and also pleased with a neighbor who lives a different lifestyle.

So, what shall we classify as sin? How do we know if we are pleasing God or living in a manner displeasing to Him? God is the creator of all things, including you and me. I think He expects us to love and honor Him as Creator and to respect and protect all He created.

I particularly appreciate one thing Jesus said when asked about man's primary obligation to God. He said that we should love God with all of our heart, soul, mind, and strength and love our neighbor as ourselves. Many people quote that scripture, but misunderstand it. We must first love God. Second, we must love ourselves. For without self-love, we degrade God's creation and are unable to love others.

Ministers often have preached that scripture (Matthew 22:37–39) giving it a negative twist regarding self. They suggest that one of the problems is concerning self. We should not think of ourselves more highly than we ought to think. However, in our society, self-exaltation does not seem to be the major problem. Most people lack in self-appreciation. If we are short on self-worth, it is very difficult, maybe impossible, to love God and our fellow humans as we should.

Spirituality starts with us as a part of God's creative evolution. If we love Him, love ourselves, and love all of His creation, I believe we please Him immensely. However, if we fail to love ourselves—and the rest of His wonderful work—no doubt we disappoint the Creator.

A good and godly life, without all the "religious hodgepodge," is, I think, loving the Creator and all He created, through word and deed.

Questions and Points to Ponder

- Why would the same God we acknowledge in the story of the prodigal son be so harsh to Adam and Eve?

- Do you think God would deliberately set up Adam and Eve in a no-win situation?

- Does reading the *National Geographic* article about the woman's skull found in Ethiopia—and estimated to be a million years old—help you to put the Genesis story in perspective?

- Does the curse of original sin do damage to our self-worth?

- Would it be advisable for us to teach that all of God's creation is wonderful, including us, and that our primary duty is to remain good and just and kind?

Chapter VI:

Gods

Early in life, I was taught about God. The teachings were simple, easy, and Biblical. God is our heavenly Father. He created all things. He is in all places, at all times, but primarily He resides in heaven. He watches over us individually. He knows our actions, thoughts, every move, and mood. He knows everything about us all the time. According to Matthew 10:30, "The very hairs of your head are all numbered."

The idea that God was always watching troubled me as a youth. I wondered if God saw Grandma Sago with her teeth out. Did He see Grandpa walking home from the store when he had a little too much to drink? Did God see and care about the married man from the neighboring town who drove down our street every Thursday night, about nine, to visit the lady who lived at the bottom of the hill? As I got older and involved in sports at the high school, I wondered if God saw and heard all that goes on in the locker room. I concluded that if He did, He understood.

God is God! That's the way it is! That's the way it is told in the book of Genesis. That's the way it has always been and is today. There was nothing before God. After all, Genesis proclaimed, "In the beginning was God." There was nothing else, just God! That's what I believed, and so did most of the other folks in my hometown. But, can it be true?

Who is God? Where is God? Is it possible to know Him? In my early teens, I knew all the answers to these big questions. I had been told by my folks, neighbors, Sunday school teachers, and the preacher. As a college sophomore, I knew even more about God, details about what he expected of me, and how I should serve Him. In seminary, I was an absolute authority on God. As a young pastor, I told others the answers. Now, in my late seventies, I often wonder if I even know the questions. What does God really expect of me? As Mark Twain often said, "I would give worlds to know."

It seems obvious that the earliest human beings also wondered about God. Their ponderings resulted in many concepts of deities. The earliest gods predate the written word. Evidence is found in symbols, pottery vessels, and cosmetic palettes. Some of the earliest signs relating to belief in gods are found in Egypt in the form of animals, particularly gazelles, jackals, and cattle. Most worship of animal-like deities appears to precede the documented kings of Egypt, who themselves were considered to be objects of worship, claiming ancestors who came from other worlds. Between 3000 and 2800 BC, about the time that the Egyptians began to write, worship became more directed toward images that initially resembled human beings—animals with human heads or an animal head on a human body.

Greek gods were primarily in human form and usually it was assumed that they were a part of a family of gods and performed many functions. For example, Apollo, the son of Jupiter and the Greek god of music, was also the god of medicine and the god of truth.

In early Rome, gods were better described as divine manifestations: spiritual beings with no human form, something similar to our concept of the Holy Spirit. The idea of gods resembling human beings came later, probably after the introduction of ideology from Egypt and Greece. The Romans had many gods, chief among them Jupiter, the king of gods; Hera, the queen of gods; Pluto, the god of death; and Diana, goddess of the moon.

For the Greeks and Romans, there seemed to be a rather simple formula regarding the number of gods. When they were unable to explain or control any situation such as weather, change of seasons, natural disasters, the sun or the moon, that gave reason for the creation of a new god. Pascal is credited with having said, "Man is surely crazy; he can't make a worm, but he makes gods by the dozen."

Because Egypt, Greece, and Rome had many gods, they were labeled polytheistic. Every part of the universe seemed to give reason for the appointment of another god. If they didn't understand something, they thanked a god or blamed it on a god. Now, in the twenty-first century, although most people would not admit to it, there is a tendency toward polytheism. We tend to quietly worship many things: money, beauty, and stuff. As the comedian George Carlin pointed out, we accumulate stuff, display our stuff, and when we have more stuff than we can handle in one place, we store our stuff. We build houses like castles far larger than needed for any practical purposes in living. Our palaces become idols of pride and, to some extent, worship.

Into the ancient world of many gods came a new nation of Israel. The religion of Israel was Judaism and primarily the teaching of one God. In principle, Israel was monotheistic: serving one God and one God only. Thus, the first commandment of Judaism is:

"I am the Lord your God ... you shall have no other gods before Me. You shall not make for yourself an idol or any likeness of what is in heaven above or in the earth beneath or in the water beneath the earth." (Exodus 20:2–4)

According to Jewish history, God spoke to Abraham, instructing him to:

"Go forth from your country and from your relatives and from your father's house, to a land which I will show you; and I will make you a great nation and I will bless you and make your name great and so you shall be a blessing; and I will bless those who

bless you and the one who curses you I will curse;
and all the families of the earth shall be blessed."
(Genesis 12:1–3)

So Abraham, at age seventy-five, with his wife, Sarah, and his nephew, Lot, along with their servants and herdsmen, set out from Ur, approximately the area of present Bagdad, to a place unknown.

Abraham is credited with being the father of the Jewish nation of Israel. Most importantly, he also brought to Israel the philosophy of only one God (i.e., absolute monotheism).

As a nation and as a religious society, Israel seemed to be caught between "the devil and the deep blue sea." To its south was the powerful nation of Egypt, with strong armies and many gods to guide them; to the far north the Roman Empire, which grew to surround the Mediterranean Sea like a great dragon. So, there stood small Israel, a new country, rebuffing the gods of the strongest and largest countries on earth.

Israel continually proclaimed that there was and is only one God. To substantiate that claim, Jewish leaders wrote books for Jews to instruct and control them in their religion and their daily activity. These books eventually became identified as the Pentateuch of the Old Testament: Genesis, Exodus, Leviticus, Numbers, and Deuteronomy.

The people of Israel define God as the Being who created all things, whether on earth or in the heavens. He now rules over his universe. God is holy, just, sovereign, omnipotent, omniscient, omnipresent, gracious, and giving. He is eternal and unaffected by earthly forces.

Judaism teaches that God is neither spirit nor matter. This, of course raises another question—if not spirit or matter, then what? Their teachings offer a partial answer: God is neither matter nor spirit because he created both. They believe that God has two distinct personalities: God Himself, who is completely unknowable, and that part which God may reveal in order to interact with his universe.

Religions became more complicated with the addition of earthly representatives of God, most notable among them Jesus and

Mohammed. Due to the teachings of the representatives, Islam and Christianity became opposing forces, as did Islam and Judaism. Judaism and Christianity are not in total opposition, although they differ greatly over the place of Christ as representative in the scheme of God's plan.

The coming of Christ and His teachings concerning Himself and God the Father complicated all things religious. His teachings and the interpretations thereof have become Christian doctrine, which states that God is a single Being in three persons: the Father, the Son, and the Holy Spirit. The Trinity, a concept first articulated in the early fourth century at the Council of Nicaea, is defined as the Father as the creator of all things, the source of all light, having all power, all knowledge and being beyond time; the Son, Jesus Christ, both God and man, the redeemer and savior of mankind; and the Holy Spirit, a continuing presence and advocate for mankind.

A problem for many believers is that Trinitarianism—the Father, the Son, and the Holy Spirit—seems to be more closely related to polytheism than monotheism. It took many centuries to move from the many gods of Egypt, Greece, and Rome to the one God of Israel. Now, in newly formed Christianity, there seemed to be three again. Is there really a difference between three Gods as opposed to one God with three rather distinct functions?

Muslims contend that God is one—perfect in every way, self-sufficient, omnipotent, and omniscient. The God of Islam does not necessarily resemble any of his creations. I am told that the Koran includes ninety-nine different names for God. (Admittedly, I did not actually read them all.) The holy writings of Islam make no attempt to describe God.

The large and looming question is whether we can know God. Can we describe God? Both the Hebrew Old Testament and the Christian New Testament describe God in numerous ways, primarily having human form. There is reference to the mind of God, the hands of God, God walking and talking. There are numerous references to the heart of God, giving the image of a human-like heavenly Being that both created and controls the universe. Some Christian writers contend that God has human-like emotions such as anger and jealousy. Others refer to attributes such as loving kindness, patience, and suffering as being characteristics of God. At the same time, the New Testament contends that "God is spirit; and those who worship Him must worship in spirit and truth" (John 4:24). There seems to be a lack of consistency in the Biblical descriptions of God.

It may be most consistent with logic, history, and all theological study simply to say, "God is." According to linguistic definition, "is" is a verb indicating a presence or being. On the other hand, God, according to all philosophical thought, existed long before language. Perhaps there is no definition. Could it be that we need no definition?

It may be that the names we have given God make everything more confusing. In early Jewish scriptures, God is primarily referred to as Jehovah or Elohim. Christians use the word God, but they tend to believe, or at least state, that "God was in Christ." Islam believes that God worked in and through Mohammed. Could it be that naming God is a big mistake, given that He is eternal, omnipotent, and omniscient? Perhaps God is simply enough. Why should we dispute definitions and titles when so much is at stake?

Thoughts of this nature may have caused the Old Testament writer, who was telling of Moses being prepared to go into Egypt to lead the Children of Israel out of bondage, to say,

> I am going to the sons of Israel, and I shall say to them, "The God of your fathers has sent me." Now they may say to me "What is His name?" And God said to Moses, "Say to the sons of Israel, I *am* has sent me to you." (Exodus 3:14)

Maybe that writer thought then as I am thinking now. God is actually too big for any single name or description that the human mind may conceive.

Since recorded history, and perhaps long before, man seems to have created gods, largely in an attempt to give answers to the mysteries of life—if not answers, certainly reasons or causes for the things he could not understand. "It is the will of the gods," or "it is an act of the gods" have been given as explanations for unforeseen circumstances ranging from untimely deaths or human acts of violence to natural disasters.

Just before writing this chapter, I watched a television program about a woman who was sent to prison for killing her husband with multiple stab wounds. She was seeking a second trial that could reduce her term or free her altogether. During the prison interview she said, "It's all in God's plan." She seemed to be using God as an excuse for her very serious predicament; she was in big trouble! As a consolation to herself, she reasoned, if only for that moment, that she and her predicament were a part of the plan of the great "I am." I wonder.

Questions and Points to Ponder

- Is it necessary to describe God in any way? Do we need a name other than God?

- Does it upset you to realize that the Egyptians, Romans, and other societies had hundreds of gods, some of them long before the Lord God Jehovah?

- Why do you suppose that God called Abraham— if, in fact he did—to go to the land of Israel and proclaim that there is one God and one God only?

- In your opinion, do representatives of God muddy the "spiritual waters"? Without Christ, Mohammed, and other representatives, could we all worship God and only God?

- Is Christianity advanced by being ultra exclusive (i.e., "the only way")?

Chapter VII:

My God Is Wonderful!

Teachings during my most formative years caused me to believe that God is sort of a human-like "Big Man" in the sky. Beyond that, God watches me, taking notes about my activities, underlining my wrongdoings, and preserving a copy for Judgment Day. I think that it would be safe to say that I was taught to fear God. It has taken decades for me to erase the notions that brought fear and replace them with a view of absolute wonder. The following represents my view of God as I near the end of eight decades.

Throughout this writing, I refer to God in the masculine gender (i.e., Father and He). I am fully aware that many of the traits of God, such as loving kindness, unwavering love, and to some extent continuing creativity, may be more feminine and that many people prefer the term, Mother-Father God. I am in complete agreement with the mothering instinct of God. However, perhaps in part, due to my age, I continue to refer to God as He.

God is wonderful and real! His creation is magnificent! His formation of mountains and canyons, lakes and rivers, and oceans and continents are beyond the realm of human comprehension. I see God everywhere: in the ants that crawl around our porch, the crickets in the garage, the beautiful dove that is nesting on our patio, the finches that sing so beautifully, the rain, the wind, beautiful cloud formations, the sunshine, and sometimes the storm. It is all God. Thankfully, that is the way I see things now.

For many years, God was primarily my taskmaster. I was a minister of several churches, and for thirty-five years, I was an administrator in church-related colleges and universities. The pressure to balance the budget, raise money through giving, support the doctrine of the particular organization, and to always act religious seemed unreal and cold. I found that many people involved in religious organizations made an attempt to be pristine and precise, but sometimes they actually seemed distant. The majority of people I met in religious organizations seemed to have closed minds regarding religious matters. What they had been told or what they had read, combined with the rules of the organization, became the fact, not to be discussed, or questioned. Often my work was more duty than joy.

Still, I enjoy speaking with Christians; however, I am continually aware that many religious people, even in friendly conversation, listen closely to make sure that the selected vocabulary is in tune with their belief system. The whole process seems to create something less than perfect love and fellowship. It causes us to feel religiously uptight—even among friends.

I remember when spirituality, not religion, began to be relaxing for me. My faith became fun. God became more real, more present, and more loving. At the same time, I was able to find myself and I, too, became more real. God had not changed—I did!

Without the everyday grind of a religious organization—its projects and prohibitions—I began to think more about God, not His messengers. More than ever, I am intrigued with His creation, not as in Genesis, but his creation of all things, and His continued governance over His natural laws. Life became better and free and more spiritual when I centered my life in God.

But now I have a problem. I am not truly Protestant. I am not Catholic, Jewish, Muslim, or Buddhist. I am a Deist. I believe in God. I believe in God supremely. I believe that God is the divine Creator and Ruler of the universe. His Being is substantiated through reason and observation of the natural world without the need for faith or churches or other religious organizations to explain and direct.

I do not believe that God involves Himself directly in the day-to-day functions of the natural world. He allows it to run according to the laws He established during creation. I believe that He is proud of us as His creation and trusts us to deal with ourselves and all other things created by Him. Naturally, our job is easier if we acknowledge Him at all times. It comforts me to believe that God is consistent and that His laws are the same day after day. The laws of nature do not change because of a prayer, be the petitioner the pope or a saintly grandmother.

While visiting a federal office in Washington DC, I chuckled heartily at a large cartoon posted on a bulletin board. The drawing, about three feet high, showed a New York skyscraper with a view from the top downward, as if the viewer was looking down from space. Two men had jumped off the building and were falling toward the concrete pavement below. One descender spoke to the other on the way down, asking, "Shall we try for coverage or penetration?" I found that cartoon very entertaining. However, in a sense, it was sobering. It reminds us that God's laws are not altered by our whims and notions, religious or otherwise; the law of gravity does not change.

None of God's created matter is ever permanently lost; it only changes in form. Some of the greatest changes are caused by man's thoughtless dabbling with His creation. We shoot carbon into the air, cause oil spills in our great oceans, killing fish and birds and, in all probability, at some point, larger animals and humans. Then, there are wars. Seemingly, never-ending wars!

I am a Deist because I believe solely in God. That belief requires no doctrinal governance or precise definitions. Deists believe that there is only one Supreme Being. He is, at the same time, both mysteriously personal and distant from the world. He remains actively interested in us—and all His creation. God considers the created to be self-sustaining. Consequently, He does not intervene in every petty personal or even life-changing cause for which we may pray. Both birth and death are good, and life between the two is wonderful. Life—the short time between birth and death—defines one's real belief in, and appreciation for, the Creator.

Deism first became recognized as a belief system during the seventeenth century, sometimes called "the Age of Enlightenment." It seems that most early Deists, especially in the United States, France, and England, were people who had been raised as Protestant Christians but upon reaching maturity found that they could not believe in such things as a triune God, the inerrancies of the Bible, the divinity of Christ, and miracles that were so far outside the natural order. The first Deists did not form congregations, but after a few hundred years, such groups as Unitarianism and Universalism came about as the result of deistic belief.

Most early Deists were considered by Christian writers of the time to be atheists. Some Deists rejected miracles and prophesies, but considered themselves to be Christians because they believed in what they considered to be the purest form of Christianity. Christianity, as they explained it, existed for some time before it was corrupted by the addition of prophecies, miracles, and the doctrine of the trinity. The same Deists, for the most part, rejected Jesus as one with God, but held that He was a man of godly virtues and a great teacher of morality. Such teachings can be found in Thomas Jefferson's *Jefferson Bible* or Matthew Tyndale's *Christianity as Old as the Creation*.

As the result of my research, I have concluded that the guiding elements that define deistic thought are:

- God exists; He is as real as His creation. God created and governs the universe.

- God created humans, perhaps through long evolution of the species. Whatever the process, He created within them the ability to reason.

- God desires that His created humans behave lovingly toward each other and morally at all times.

- Deism largely rejects all religions that are based on "the direct revealed word of God."

- Deists do not believe in miracles, prophecies, or religious mysteries. They believe that the laws of nature, created by God, continue without exception.

One of the early English Deists was Lord Herbert of Cherbury. He contended that there are five common factors in religion:

- There is one supreme God.

- He ought to be worshipped.

- Adoration and piety are the chief parts of divine worship.

- We ought to be sorry for our sins and repent of them.

- Divine goodness doth dispense rewards and punishments, both in this life and after it.

(John Orr, *English Deism,* page 62)

Well-known Deists in history include Matthew Tyndale, Voltaire, David Hume, and Thomas Payne. Some American founding fathers were apparently influenced by deism, including Thomas Jefferson and Benjamin Franklin. Other notable founding fathers may have been more truly classified as Deists, including James Madison, John Adams, and possibly Alexander Hamilton. Historians have argued for several centuries whether our founding fathers were Christians, Deists, or some mix of the two.

Being a Deist solves a lot of the problems that I have mentally wrestled with for most of my life. Chief among those is prayer. People all around the world pray. In the same geographic area, some may be praying for cooler weather because it is too hot; others may be thanking God for the heat. Some may pray for rain, while others do not need or want rain. People's needs, wants, and notions seem to vary according to the number of people involved.

Most contemporary Deists believe that God created a perfect universe. No amount of prayer by anyone can change the fundamental nature of God's creation. Other Deists believe that God cannot be contacted at all through prayer. They believe that God is only experienced through the wonder of His creation. Some Deists find value in prayer as a form of meditation, although they do not believe in divine intervention. For Deists, prayer is more of a "thank you" as opposed to "God grant to me."

For me, the basis of deism is belief in our magnificent Creator. That belief, then, must be shown through our everyday acts of appreciation for His creation. God does not need our help in His control or maintenance of the universe. To my knowledge, He has never asked for suggestions. But He does, I know, delight in our appreciation.

Questions and Points to Ponder

- Is your religion a joy? Do you sometimes tire of playing a religious role? Is your God a judge or a friend and loving heavenly Father?

- Is your faith fun? Do you feel joy in being a part of God's creation?

- Are your prayers primarily requests or thanksgiving?

- Is it necessary to go to church or any other particular place to worship God? Does God give you gold stars for church attendance?

Chapter VIII:

Afterlife

I was told about heaven when just a child. "God is watching you from heaven," or "Good boys and girls go to heaven." In church, we sang songs about meeting in heaven: "In the Sweet By and By," "Meeting on the Beautiful Shore," etc. In religion, particularly Christianity, heaven is a major subject of conversation and anticipation.

It is generally agreed that human beings are the only animals who think logically and futuristically. Also, I think humans are the only beings so egotistical in their thinking that they cannot imagine life being only that time between birth and death. It seems that humans consider themselves to be so much above all other animals, so advanced, so important, that there is only one logical conclusion—they must be eternal!

The afterlife, also referred to as life after death, the next world, or the hereafter, is embraced by most, regardless of nationality, color, or creed. There seems to be a prevailing thought that there must be more than this present plane of existence. I assume that views of the afterlife came naturally and possibly as far back as cavemen looking at the stars and considering the awesomeness of space. For them, the beyond was only to be viewed with wonder. Probably they considered the beyond to be unattainable. Then, after time, came organized religion and metaphysics. Many religious people spend a great deal of their time thinking, reading, and singing about the hereafter. It is very common, particularly here in the Bible Belt, to hear such words as these after a death: "She is in a better place," or "He is now with his mother and dad and Jesus in heaven." I believe that more people are drawn to religion because of their fascination for—or fear of—the afterlife than for any other reason.

Beyond our belief in the hereafter, most people—largely as the result of religious teachings—believe that our existence following death is determined by God, based on one's life while here on earth. Most religions, but not all, believe that the afterlife is spent in either heaven for the righteous and chosen of God, or hell, for those who sin against or fail to acknowledge God.

There seems to be two very differing views of the afterlife: religious views based on faith, and empirical views based on logic and observation. Most religious people have a belief in the hereafter based on faith. Faith comes from teachings by the church, ancestral views handed down through families, or perhaps faith stories from the Bible and other religious books such as the Talmud. Others take a more logical approach toward the hereafter. Their observations are based on reason, parapsychology, and psychic research that sometimes include interviews, studies of out-of-body or near-death experiences, and mediumship.

Most people believe in some form of afterlife. Some believe in an afterlife with God. Buddhists tend to believe in afterlife, but without any reference to God. The Sadducees, early Jewish religious leaders, believed firmly in God, but held no belief in an afterlife. Christians believe that the soul continues after death in either heaven or hell. Hindus and Buddhists tend to believe in reincarnation in various human and animal forms: that one's existence in the afterlife is a reward or punishment for their conduct during life. Agnostics insist that the existence of a soul in the afterlife is not scientifically or otherwise verifiable and is, therefore, unknowable. Atheists generally believe that there is insufficient evidence for any type of existence after death.

As we think about the afterlife, let's confine our considerations to Protestant and Catholic Christian views resulting from Biblical study and interpretation.

Generally, there are three views in Christianity. The conservative Protestant view is that those who believe in Jesus Christ and are "saved" will go to heaven. Those who do not accept Jesus as the "Way, the Truth, and the Life," will endure extreme torture in hell. Liberal Christians do not usually believe in hell as a physical place, but rather that punishment is mental anguish over a life misspent.

The Roman Catholic view differs somewhat from either liberal or conservative Protestant teachings. Catholic doctrine contends that very few people will experience direct entry into heaven. Those whose sins have been forgiven through church ritual will go to purgatory for a process of mellowing and cleansing after death. Later they may be allowed into heaven. All others who have not been forgiven through rituals of the church will go directly to hell, a state of existence where inhabitants will suffer torment forever.

Let's further consider the belief patterns of liberal and conservative Christians and Roman Catholics. Conservative Protestants believe that the Bible gives an adequate reason to substantiate an afterlife, and that every person has eternal life someplace. Eternity will be spent in one of two God-created places. Heaven is seen as a place where there will be no pain, disease, depression, or death. People will live in new spiritual bodies and enjoy the companionship of Christ forever in a place that John, in the Book of the Revelation, described as having pearly gates, streets of gold, crystal seas, mansions, and eternal peace and joy for its citizens.

Conservatives may be adjusting their beliefs concerning hell. A growing number seem to believe that hell is not a place of physical punishment, but complete isolation from God. However, fundamentalists insist that hell is a place of intense torture with no relief through eternity. Others in the conservative camp tend to believe in what has been loosely defined as conditionalism (i.e., those in hell will probably be punished in proportion to their sins while here on earth).

Liberal Christians hold a variety of beliefs about heaven and hell and the hereafter. Most of their beliefs are based on logic and their opinion concerning the nature of God. Liberal Christians tend to believe that hell does not exist as a place of eternal punishment. At best, hell is a concept, not a place. Liberals object to only the saved being rewarded, rationalizing that it is unjust to punish a person who has never heard the gospel. Most liberal Christians also believe that people of differing beliefs can enjoy the love of God and his favor in the hereafter, if such exists. The bottom line for liberals is that a loving God would be incapable of creating a place of torture for his creation.

While I make no claim of being an expert on Catholic theology, my understanding of the teaching of the Roman Catholic Church concerning the hereafter is that there is a belief in both heaven and hell. However, as previously mentioned, Catholics believe in purgatory, an intermediate stop where believers may be fully cleansed and made acceptable for admission into heaven. The wicked will go to hell and suffer torment along with Satan and his angels. In the case of babies who die before baptism, Catholic doctrine seems a bit ambivalent, according to official pronouncements. However, although it is not Catholic doctrine, many Catholics believe that newborns go to a state defined as "limbo," not heaven, but a place where the infants will be happy and at peace.

So, what shall we say about the hereafter? At best, it is a mystery. Belief in future existence seems to be troubling for some and a cause of contentment for others.

After years of consideration of this matter, I have decided to live as best I can; thus, if there is an afterlife, I will enjoy it. In the meantime, I greatly love and appreciate the wonderful creations of God in the here and now.

Questions and Points to Ponder

- How important is belief in an afterlife to your daily activities and personal well-being?

- Does it sometimes seem that you are living primarily for a reward?

- Do you think that most people would have the same religious fervor if death was the end?

- Is it logical to think that God keeps "tabs" on us (i.e., like Santa Claus, he checks when we are good or bad)?

- Does your image of God include a being or spirit that is anxious to punish?

Chapter IX:

Hell

My first exposure to the very idea of hell was not at any of the three churches I frequently attended. I heard a lot about hell at Grandpa's saloon. It was not uncommon for a man to come into the bar, throw his hat on the rack, and exclaim, "Bill, it's as hot as hell!" Of course in the winter, it was as cold as hell. At times when there was an argument between a couple at the bar, one might tell the other to go to hell. So, as a kid, I really didn't know if hell was cold or hot or a place where one went voluntarily or by invitation only. But I did hear a lot about hell.

"Everyone is going to hell, according to *someone's* religion." As troubling as that common statement may be, I think it represents the harshness of some religions and the reality of the vastly varied views among church organizations. Another truism is that hell is the place of punishment prepared by God for someone else.

In the previous chapter, we discussed hell as a place of suffering and punishment in the afterlife. Hell is traditionally depicted as fiery and painful. However, in some traditions, hell is portrayed as cold and gloomy. As I remember, Dante's *Inferno* portrays the innermost circle of hell as a frozen lake of blood and guilt. Most religious groups that believe in hell are also convinced that it is the residence of the devil and his angels.

Hell appears in several mythologies and ancient religions and has often been depicted in art and literature. Primarily the Christian doctrine of hell is derived from the New Testament where hell is described by the Greek word, Hades, or the Arabic word, Gehenna. Hades has similarities to the Old Testament term Sheol as "the place of the dead" or the grave. Therefore, in the strictest view, Sheol would be the final abode of both the wicked and the righteous, since all eventually die.

Gehenna has been the most misused term to describe a place of torment. The word refers to the Valley of Hinnon, which was a garbage dump outside Jerusalem. It was a place where the residents burned their trash, so there always seemed to be a fire burning at Hinnon. Gehenna is used in the New Testament as a metaphor for a burning place of punishment for the wicked.

Jesus referred to Gehenna with regard to punishment for a life poorly lived. It could be that His intent was to suggest that we must live useful, productive lives of service and kindness. Otherwise, our lives may become useless, like trash for the dumps of Gehenna.

Much has been said about hell in Chapter VIII and a great deal more could be discussed without exhausting resources. However, it is not my purpose here to discuss whether there is or is not a place called hell. Rather, I would have you think more about the nature of God. Would He, in the wildest stretch of human imagination, create a place of torture and eternal pain for his created? For me, it seems best and right to describe my God as a loving, merciful Father who cares for His children. As suggested in the New Testament, if earthly men (fathers) know how and wish to do good for their children, how much more will our heavenly Father do for us!

Why do you suppose we give so much attention to the subject of hell? Obviously, it is not a desirable place. It is a state or condition about which we would rather not think and certainly a destination we would not choose. Consider that in most every state, there are several correctional institutions and prisons. Inside prison walls, there are murderers, thieves, rapists, druggies, and all sorts of demented personalities. This I say with full knowledge that occasionally, with the limitations of our justice system, there could be an innocent person there, too. However, my point is that there may be a prison just outside my city's limits; however, I do not concern myself regularly with the threat or the notion that I may end up in prison someday. Even though the place is real and the concept seemingly necessary, if I live my life honestly, uprightly, and within the law of both God and man, I have no reason or cause to concern myself with the prison so close at hand. So it should be with our consideration of hell.

Why, then, are most people so concerned about the impending torture of hell? Probably it has to do with our previously discussed topic of original or inherited sin. Do you remember the day I went to the rock to confess my sins because an evangelist had told me that I was headed for hell on a slippery slope? When I sat down on the rock to pray, obviously hell was a factor in my mind. My mental condition and emotions were akin to driving by the gates of the local prison, always expecting a guard to run out and pull me in, even though I had no idea of wrongdoing.

Of all the doctrines held by churches, I find the belief in hell to be one of the most perplexing. Such a belief suggests that God is vengeful and anxious to judge His creation and to condemn them— not only to death, but to a fiery place where they will burn forever. Many Christians seem content to wrestle with the idea of hell. Their religious goal of life is to gain heaven and escape hell. I think that the whole idea is implanted by well-meaning preachers and evangelists who find some reward in frightening and intimidating their people in order to gain converts, greater loyalty to the church, and of course, more gifts in the offering plates.

Some TV evangelists depict God as being very angry and impatient with people. Sometimes I turn on the TV, find such an evangelist, and then turn the sound completely off. It is amazing to watch the body language of such spokesmen for religion. Their facial muscles become rigid and tense as they describe the fury of God's judgment. Perhaps it is in frustration that they attribute to Him traits of their own humanity and anger, not realizing that God is far beyond and above our pettiness, wrath, anger, depression, and the human urge to "get even."

This reminds me of an old story I heard in seminary. A professor in a class on preaching was explaining to a rather awkward young man the importance of emotion and expression during the sermon. He said, "When you are preaching on heaven, let your eyes light up, smile, stand erect and proud. Then, when you are preaching about hell, your normal expression will be adequate."

Prior to July 1999, the Catholic Church taught that hell is a location where its population will be punished without hope of relief for eternity. Among the inmates in hell will be Satan and his angels and all persons who have died with "grave and unrepented sins," that have not been cleansed by church rituals. The level of torture in hell will be in accordance with the seriousness of the individual's sin.

On Wednesday, July 28, 1999, during a general audience, Pope John Paul II made the following statements that hit the front pages of many newspapers around the world:

"Hell is not a punishment imposed externally by God, but a condition resulting from attitudes and actions which people adopt in this life ... so eternal damnation is not God's work but is actually our own doing ... More than a physical place, hell is the state of those who freely and definitively separate themselves from God."

He concluded by pronouncing that hell is "the pain, frustration, and emptiness of life without God."

It is not surprising that Pope John Paul was the most widely accepted and appreciated pontiff in the long history of the Catholic Church.

Questions and Points to Ponder

- Have you pondered this matter? Our belief concerning reward and punishment may have more to do with our concept of the character of God than a place.

- Is it consistent with belief in a loving God to believe that He created, in advance, a place of torture and punishment?

- Does it trouble you that some Protestant faiths believe that souls are destined for reward or punishment even before birth?

- Do you agree with me that we give the devil more credit than he deserves?

- If hell is an actual place, where would it be? Could it be a state in which we are now living?

Chapter X:

Heaven

For most religious people, the term "heaven" represents not only a hope and longing for the continuance of life, but a physical plane of existence in the afterlife. The New Testament makes many references to heaven and uses several descriptive names, including "the Kingdom of Heaven," "the City of God," and "the New Jerusalem."

Some churches teach that one enters heaven immediately at the time of death. The New Testament suggests that when we are absent from the body, we are present with God. Other religions contend that entry into heaven follows the resurrection and Day of Judgment. Simply stated, the Christian belief is that if we accept Christ as our personal Savior, having sins forgiven, heaven will be our eternal home.

After long consideration, I have determined that heaven is what we would like for it to be. For every great trial in life, there is a heaven awaiting. After a week of trouble and agony and divisions in the family, people go to church and sing, "When we all get to heaven, what a day of rejoicing that will be!"

I often think of the Negro spirituals that relate to heaven and the conditions that prompted their writing. During slavery, many were forced to pick cotton barefoot in the hot noonday sun and would step on sharp cotton bolls. Obviously, there was a need for shoes to protect them. So came the song, "I got shoes, you got shoes, all

God's children got shoes. When I get to heaven, gonna put on my shoes and walk all over God's heaven."

Most of the cotton picking was done Monday through Saturday. Sunday was usually a day of rest and worship for the slaves. Thus, the song, "Every Day Will Be Sunday By and By."

In the Book of the Revelation, John, the writer, was in exile on the Island of Patmos. He was a prisoner; there were no guards, but he couldn't get off the island. He was a captive of the surrounding sea. So, when John described heaven, he said that there would be a crystal sea. In other words, one that could be walked upon. Other descriptions of heaven speak of mansions. That gave great hope to poor folks who were itinerant sheepherders and farm workers. The streets of gold were another part of heaven, according to John, that made the entire hope of getting there very attractive, particularly for people who struggled in poverty.

In the stormy Midwest and South, where tornadoes are always a threat in the springtime, people sang the comforting words, "Oh the land of cloudless skies; oh the land of an unclouded day."

Growing up in the Ozarks of Missouri, where most men worked hard in the lead mines, it seemed that the favorite song in our little church was "I'm Gonna Sit Down and Rest a Little While" in a place where there will be "no troubles and trials."

So, what is heaven? It is what we need most. Where is it? It is far away from a hurtful condition. For the laborer, heaven is rest; for the poor, it is gold; and for the barefoot workers, it is a place where there are shoes. It is what we would find most helpful and rewarding.

In my hometown, just five houses up the street from my birthplace, there was a well-known man who had a barbershop in the front room of his house. His name was Peg Randolph. I never knew his real first name. He had a wooden leg, so he carried the nickname of Peg. Peg gave me my first haircut, but that is not the reason that I remember him so affectionately.

Peg jumped around the barber chair on his good leg and the peg part sort of swung back and forth. I would go up to the barbershop on Saturday afternoon and get in line. It was not so much a line as a group of chairs and Peg always knew who was next. I loved being there, listening to the conversations of the neighborhood men. Admittedly, I was not there for a haircut, but to have a place in line. I loved hearing Peg say, "Sonny, you're next!" Then I would sell my place for a nickel or sometimes "two bits."

Watching Peg move around the chair and clip hair was not all there was of interest in that shop. Peg chewed tobacco. I am not referring to the sweet stuff, the snuff-like goodies that are available today. Peg chewed plug tobacco; it came in a cake about the size of a brownie. The fun part was when Peg spit all the way across the room—sometimes over the shoulder of the person in the chair—at a spittoon in the corner. Just a quick look at the walls near the corner gave evidence that Peg was not always the most accurate spitter.

Why am I telling you so much about Peg Randolph? Because Peg was the first person I had known and admired who died. I remember asking my mother where Peg went. She said, "Son, Peg's in heaven." I had visions of Peg walking around heaven with two good legs, but the rest of him was the same. As I pictured him there, I always wondered whether this old Missourian would spit tobacco on a street of gold. Or, maybe there was a special place for people like Peg, perhaps a spittoon in paradise!

It is not that I wish to make light of heaven, but I do think that all of us spend far too much time talking about avoiding hell and getting to heaven. Maybe we should spend more time enjoying the present wonders of God. We are blessed to live among God's marvelous creations: beautiful fields of wheat, tall mountains, majestic sunsets, and golden hues above an early sunrise. Our world is filled with wonder, but we become so accustomed, so preoccupied, that often we miss it all. I think it was Peter Marshall who prayed before Congress and asked the Lord to "save us from being so heavenly minded that we are no earthly good." To that I would say, Amen!

Questions and Points to Ponder

- While the hope of heaven is comforting, do you think it detracts from our appreciation of God's wonders all around us now?

- Is it possible to live such a life of thanksgiving and amazement of all of God's wonders that we can have a taste of heaven here?

- Is heaven a place or condition?

- Was Peter Marshall right? Is it possible to become "so heavenly minded that we are no earthly good"?

- If heaven is a place, given our increased knowledge of the universe, where would it be? Of course, up is no longer a logical answer.

Chapter XI:

Churchianity

I've been thinking about some of the interesting words commonly used by older folks during my boyhood in the Ozarks. For instance, when something was absolutely baffling, a problem with no obvious solution, they would often call it a "conundrum." I still like that word. It means something very puzzling and mysterious, something near unsolvable. But I think it implies even more (i.e., a mystery has a certain exciting fascination that accompanies it, and puzzles have pieces that fit together for a satisfying finish). However, a conundrum is a big problem that seems to evade solution. I say all of this in the hope of making one very sharp and painful observation. I think that organized religion is a conundrum.

How many times have you heard a friend or an associate say, "When my family gets together, there are two things we dare not discuss: religion and politics." Isn't it interesting that the two things that should most improve the quality of our lives tend to separate us from one another and slow down the process of finding solutions to our problems.

There are two major political parties in the United States: Democrat and Republican. Obviously there are other smaller organizations, but none have become significantly influential except perhaps the Tea Party and independents, who have been more recognized in recent years. Even though politics divides us, and the very process of politics seems to slow down progress, at least the divisions are fewer and quite predictable.

On the other hand, organized religion is far more complex. Christian religion apparently started out with some very simple words by Jesus concerning "My Church." It is probable that He envisioned His followers carrying His message much as presented in the Beatitudes. However, in the near two thousand years since Jesus and His disciples walked the shores of Galilee, preaching that simple gospel, the Church that He referenced has spread around the world.

According to a recent paper that crossed my desk, there are now approximately 3,800 Christian denominations (*Christianity Today,* "General Statistics and Facts of Christianity Today.") Religion becomes far more complicated than politics and probably causes greater divisions in families, communities, and nations.

It is troubling that groups that originally started with an aim to follow the Great Commission (i.e., "Go into all the world and preach the gospel") have become so divided in aim and purpose. Someone, I am not sure of the source, once said, "People who started out to be fishers of men are now keepers of the aquarium." That condition has recently been defined as "churchianity." That's a conundrum.

Divisions in religion are evident to the point of depression. If you ask someone a simple question such as, "What are your religious views?" you will probably get an answer such as, "I am Presbyterian," or "I am Baptist," etc. Most people identify themselves more with an organization than they do with purpose and the Great Commission that started it all.

In some communities, there seems to be a church on every corner. Sometimes a half dozen or more congregations—originally related to the same denomination—separate over slight differences in doctrine, or possibly hurt feelings, resulting in additional property, buildings, equipment, programs, etc., all in the same city where they originally started as a single congregation.

From all of this churchianity—loyalty to a church as an organization rather than well-defined religious principles—come numerous problems. First and primary, I do not think that it was

Christ's purpose to organize worldwide religious organizations with many billions of dollars in property and massive organizational structures, with each attempting to define a certain uniqueness to justify its existence.

Religious organizations also contribute to political problems. The very question of separation of church and state, a condition supposedly established by our nation's founding fathers seems laughable today. Church views are clearly announced in political campaigns. Religious pressure is notable. One particular church is reported to have spent millions of dollars to defeat Proposition 8 in California. That proposition would have permitted marriage between same-sex partners.

Churchianity seems to cause even greater problems. For instance, there is the matter of federal, state, and local taxes. Church properties are exempt from property tax. Several states are presently having severe financial difficulties, and it was recently reported that some cities are on the verge of bankruptcy, forcing them to reduce police departments and other essential services. In other states, cities have found it necessary to make drastic cuts in fire protection, services for the handicapped, the elderly, and education. In each of those states, there are billions of dollars in church-owned properties. Since those religious organizations do not pay property taxes, yet at the same time require all the services and protection of people and organizations that do, it seems to be a matter of gross inequity and unnecessary financial hardship for government.

Beyond the fairness issue and the dollars that are lost in taxation, the entire matter of the church's exemption from obligations that must be assumed by all others seems adequate evidence that there is not a separation between church and state (i.e., the state, indirectly, gives substantial financial support and advantage to religious organizations). There are, of course, other public benefit organizations that enjoy a tax-exempt status. To the extent that they exist, the problem increases.

I do not, by this discussion, intend in any way to detract from their benefits to society. However, those benefits seem to come at a greater cost than is usually recognized.

Then, of course, there is the matter of tax deductions for gifts to support religious organizations. The result is monumental financial loss to federal and state governments each year. It seems only fair to mention also that because churches do not pay property taxes and indirectly receive money from the state as the result of tax deductions for donors, both state and federal governments find it necessary to increase taxes on those who are required to pay. That includes you and me and most other individuals and profit-making organizations. If churches and other religious organizations were taxed on their property and their income, it would not be necessary for states to reduce educational opportunities, raise tuition prices at their state-run institutions, or make other cuts in services, as previously mentioned.

Even more frustrating is the reality that everyone who is a taxpayer in the United States supports religion, whether or not it is his or her choice to do so. Indirectly, the state and federal government lifts money from the taxpayer's pocket and deposits it in the churches' coffers.

Muslims and several Eastern religions have already established themselves in the United States. Even though citizens of the United States may disagree with their teachings, they, too, under our laws, have the same tax benefits as Christian organizations.

On several occasions during the past few years, particularly during political campaigns, the subject of a flat tax has been mentioned. Many people seem to like the idea of paying an established percentage of their income to the state and federal government without the concern of tax calculations and deductions for gifts, medical expenses, investment losses, etc. It is unlikely that such a favorable change in the tax structure will ever be made because it would eliminate deductions for gifts to religious and other exempt organizations. Without the advantage of tax-deductible gifts, religious organizations would find it difficult to meet their ever-expanding budgets.

It is not my intent to belittle either the church or the government. I love our nation and the theoretical constitutional principles on which it stands. However, to believe that there is a separation between church and state would require that we dispense with all intelligence and reason.

Churchianity has resulted in the church becoming big business. If all the various denominations of Christendom were to come together, and that is about as possible as my wife and I flying to Venus for dinner, that union would result in the most expansive property holder and the largest overall business in the world today. This raises what is perhaps the key question: exactly what should that business be?

Most denominations in Christianity have international, national, regional, state, and local offices. All of the various offices—from the local conference to the national headquarters—require financial support from the local churches. Consequently, in churchianity, there is a great reliance on income, not only for the local salaries, utilities, and programs, but also to pay apportionments and levies to the denominational superstructure. One congregation with which I was affiliated paid twenty-seven cents of every dollar of income as support to the various offices of the denomination. Beyond that, local memberships must pay for building programs, missions, local programs to aid in poverty, the homeless, illiteracy, disaster relief, and the like. So churchianity results in big business, supported by the wage-earners of each member household, in addition to rather generous support by the federal and state governments, as cited previously.

The greatest damage that occurs as the result of churchianity is just what the name implies. The name of Christ (Christianity) has been largely replaced by the church (churchianity); greater emphasis seems to be placed on physical things rather than spiritual, as is stated in the original purpose of most religious organizations. As one who has been involved in church organizations for more than fifty years, I am amazed at the smoothness with which this change has occurred.

It is difficult to adequately point out the damages of churchianity without seeming negative and critical. However, I think that most people, both young and old, would agree that the church has become more of a business and less a spiritual emphasis in most communities during the past several years.

The move from Christianity to churchianity will, in my opinion, result in continued loss of interest in the organized church. Christian service and the hope of heaven can never be replaced with the process of fundraising. Some churches are still very strict on certain points of doctrine, most of them meaningless to the actual living of the godly life, while others make few or no requirements and membership is less involved than joining a lodge or country club. Obviously, there are a few churches—for the most part independent mega-churches—that are thriving with a very positive message of God's love and fatherly forgiveness.

So you, the reader, may be asking, is there some hope for the church? My answer would be, probably not, unless religious organizations return from churchianity to Christianity and a greatly simplified organization. That seems less likely than finding the much talked about "wormhole" for time travel.

Questions and Points to Ponder

- Why are there so many churches in Christendom? After all, we are to "love our neighbor as ourself." If so, why wouldn't just a few churches in an average-size city be sufficient?

- Does there need to be so much infrastructure at such high cost to promote the gospel?

- Considering that our government proposes to separate church and state, should the church, like every other organization be taxed in order to pay for the various services required?

- What can we do to strengthen the local church and make it more responsive to the real spiritual needs of the people?

Chapter XII:

A Life Pleasing To God

Let us now get back to the question that started it all. "Dr. Sago, tell me how to live a godly life, and please leave out all the religious hodgepodge." I think that we have given sufficient time and space to the religious hodgepodge. However, I am sure that there are many people who largely depend on the hodgepodge as a major comfort and significant part of their religious activities.

The real question before us is how we recognize God in our lives. How do we sufficiently honor and praise Him and thereby bring comfort and meaning to our own being? Where do we start?

Let's go back five or six hundred years before the coming of Christ, long before the word "Christianity" came into existence. Religion was different, but the hodgepodge was there. People were faced with the same types of questions.

The Old Testament prophet Micah speaks directly to some of these questions, and, I think, gives workable and practical answers. I have always considered Micah to be a younger man with lots of questions. Now I admit that the younger part could be entirely wrong, but he did ask youthful questions. For instance, Micah was thinking some of the thoughts that we have been discussing. Can we really be godly? What does that mean? How do we do it? Can we buy our way into His pleasure and blessing? Is it something that we have to do as a routine and ritual? Exactly how do we go about standing before God and properly acknowledging Him?

I have heard prominent people talk about meeting the Queen of England. There were many questions in their mind. Should they smile or seem sober? Should they curtsy or bow? Would they dare kiss the back of her hand? What is the protocol for meeting the queen?

Not long ago, President Obama met an older leader of a foreign nation and he bowed. Not much, just a slight indication of a bow. It was his intent, I think, to show respect, not so much for position, but for age, which is highly honored in that particular part of the world. The American press went crazy. Why would the president of our great nation bow to any other? There was a rumble for days.

The greater question is how we come before God. We can't kiss His hand; we can't look into His eyes; we don't know which way to bow. We don't know where He is.

I dearly love the words of the prophet Micah in his sixth chapter, verses 6–8, which I will rather generously paraphrase. However, I encourage you to read it directly from the New American Standard Bible, which I think gives a great interpretation.

Micah put it this way: How do I go into the presence of God? I need to show humility. Do I bow? What do I do? Must I go to the temple or to a quiet place, perhaps to my closet? Where?

Shall I bring God a gift, perhaps burnt offerings, some of my finest yearling calves out of the north pasture? Do you suppose that would please Him? Can you imagine that God would take great delight if I brought a thousand rams and not only a few drops of olive oil for the forehead but ten thousand barrels of oil for the Lord? Would He be pleased? Would that be enough? Even a greater question is whether those gifts are appropriate. Aren't they already His?

Maybe I should do like Abraham and offer my firstborn as a sacrifice to God. The very fruit of my loins for the sins of my soul. Yet that doesn't seem right that someone else should pay for my sins. What does God really want from me?

Then Micah remembered that God has already told us what is good and what He requires of us, and it is all rather simple. It is not a bunch of religious hodgepodge. Just three easy-to-remember rules: to do justice, to love kindness, and to walk humbly with Him.

Let's think more about Micah's verse 8: "What does the Lord require of you but to do justice, to love kindness, and to walk humbly with your God." I think Micah was particularly careful in his choice of words. He advised us to "*do* justice." In Micah's view—and I agree—it is not enough just to believe in justice. We must *do* justice. We must live it!

There have been many perplexing human events in the history of our nation. Our forefathers came here from England to be free. After the establishment of the colonies, some became wealthy and brought in slaves from Africa to do their work. They believed in freedom; they struggled for freedom; but only for themselves. Their workers were slaves, not free.

There are politicians in Washington today who know very well what needs to be done in the best interest of our country and the people they represent. They know it—and I think they believe it— but they *do* politics.

The same is true in religion. We go to church and talk about loving others, bringing in a new age of caring, and following the examples of Biblical greats; yet at home and at work during the week, our humanity, including selfishness, comes forth. To do justice, I think, means just that. *Do* it!

When my boys were little, we visited their grandparents in Missouri, where there were lots of storms in the springtime. My youngest son, Brad, about four at the time, would watch the sky and if a black cloud came, he stayed very close to family. One day there was heavy thunder and lightning and Brad said to his grandmother, "Grandma, pray to the Lord that it will not storm."

Grandma said, "Okay," and went on about her work of cleaning the kitchen. Brad, not hearing any audible petition that seemed Godward, cried out, "Well then, Grandma, do it!" I think that is what Micah may have had in mind. As godly people, we must do more than think about justice or even say we believe in justice. We must *do* it.

Next, as a part of verse 8, chapter 6, Micah says we are to "love kindness." I have found that what we truly love dominates our life. It is easy to say that we love someone or something. It is easy to sing love songs about leaving your heart in a particular place or with a person, but those are just words. Micah, I think, was saying that if we love God, we will be kind to all of His creation. Kindness means to do good for, to be conscious of, to be helpful to, and to appreciate the reality of a person or thing. If we all loved kindness, there would be little or no quarreling, family fights, community disputes, and probably not even a war. If everybody loved kindness.

Finally, Micah says, "Walk humbly with your God." Humility is a trait often forgotten in our society. It seems to fade as prosperity comes. Humility involves acknowledging God more than self. I have learned, admittedly far too late in life, that humility involves understanding that the world is not mine but God's.

With all I have striven after, and perhaps gained, I still have nothing when compared to the creations of God all around me. It could be that loving God is easier as we get older. There is more time for thought and introspection. There is time to observe in a way that youthful eyes may not see.

My life goes something like this: I rise up in the morning; it is another day that God has provided for me. I look out at green trees, beautiful blue skies, sometimes a gentle rain; it is all God's. It is a blessing from God. Notice that I did not include sunrise. I know it is there, but I am seldom up in time to view it personally! That is another advantage of growing old.

Donna and I enjoy taking drives through the countryside, or, as we did recently, a drive from Oklahoma to Southern California and back. We were astounded anew with creation: majestic mountains reaching thousands of feet into the sky with sides that seem torn, exhibiting ages of weathering and layering. Through stretches of desert there was the sudden appearance of ancient lava flow. Then there were green valleys and flowing rivers. It was overwhelming and, as the day went on, there was the sunset with hues of purple, red, and orange, definitely the work of a Master Painter, the Creator, the Sustainer of everyone and everything, including us.

As mentioned earlier, one of the supreme Jewish laws was to "Love the Lord thy God with all thy heart, mind, and strength." I think Micah, with his advice, helps us to do that. Jesus added a few words to that law. "Love your neighbor as yourself." It all seems so simple and the first part is really quite easy to understand. We know that we should love our Creator with all of our being; that's a given. The difficulty comes with loving the created.

Now comes the part that most of us miss. Love your neighbor as yourself implies that first you must love yourself as a part of God's creation. He structured you in a magnificent way through creative evolution. If we are able to love ourselves as God's created, then and only then, will we be able to love our neighbors as ourselves.

So, the answer is Yes! We can live godly lives without all the religious hodgepodge. But it isn't easy, unless we intentionally think about it every day and make precise plans to do it.

Questions and Points to Ponder

- Is your religious life confusing? Would it be easier to worship God and God alone?

- A lot is said and written about "giving to God." Can we really give stuff to God? Does God need our stuff?

- Do you believe that a God of mercy and love requires sacrifice?

- What do you suppose the world would be like if we all decided to "do justice"?

- Do you find it difficult to love yourself? Perhaps self-love is the key to all loving.

Chapter XIII:

Sin Brings Big Business

After reading the previous chapters, you may be thinking that I am really hung up on Genesis 1 (i.e., creation, the fall of man, and original/inherited sin). I plead guilty. I firmly believe that the doctrine of original sin is the most damaging and damning doctrine in religion.

The doctrine of inherited sin was a good thing for the Jewish rabbis. Being tainted with sin tends to create an accompanying feeling of guilt. The rabbis played guilt to the hilt. The Old Testament explains how they required sacrifices that were supposed to temporarily bring forgiveness for sins, both inherited and committed. For small sins, a person could sacrifice turtledoves; for more grievous sins, the sacrifice required was the finest fatted calf from the flock. The doctrine also fostered a controlling element in religion that continues to this day.

The theory seems to be that you come into this world damaged and dirty; if you 'fess up, pay up, and march to the beat of the organized church, you may be forgiven.

So, it is a clear fact of history that those early Jewish rabbis and writers who concocted such a theory were not only conniving against their congregations, but they also immeasurably damaged all generations yet to come. I cannot imagine that God can be pleased with such heavy religious manipulation. Of course, we realize now that Genesis 1 is mythology. Yet, the church continues to preach the story of creation and fallen man as if it were true and God's own doing. Original sin is damning because its very existence serves as an accusation against God, suggesting a God of anger and vengeance and a Creator unwilling to forgive His highest creation.

A few weeks ago, I read about a man released from prison after serving more than twenty years for a crime he did not commit. One gasps at the very thought of such unnecessary and undeserved confinement—and may even doubt the process through which the man was originally condemned. How much more should we doubt the suggestion that God labels us with sin even before we are born? Such a theory is unthinkable. As a matter of fact, that is the reason it has survived through these several hundred years. *People fail to think.*

Throughout the centuries covered by the Old Testament writers, temple leaders continued to extract sacrifices from their people. Then came Jesus as God's messenger and the writings of the New Testament. The gospels maintain that Christ died on a cross as the final sacrifice for original sin. His death covered the guilt of every person for all time. Christ was, of course, the messenger of God.

In all religions, the messengers have always caused problems. Just to think that God finds it necessary to send a messenger to explain to us who and what He is seems absurd. God, being God, needs no assistance. The story of Christ was simply a continuation of a theory of sacrifice as forgiveness for inherited sin.

I firmly believe in Jesus Christ as an historic being. I believe that His intent and purpose was to bring justice, peace, and civility by making changes in the Jewish ideas of worship. The virgin birth, miracles, resurrection, and ascension all raise even greater questions. All these things are outside the natural order. Given the religious indoctrination over the last two thousand years, it is doubtful that any of those assumed happenings will ever be seriously questioned by the church. For without those mythologies, the Christian churches would obviously find it necessary to relate directly to God.

Imagine, as a Christian, what worship would be without the Biblical, doctrinal, and emotional references to Christ that are the major part of every service. Christ proclaimed himself to be equal with the Father. Three centuries later, the church added to the Father and Son a new part called the Holy Spirit. These eventually found their way into the New Testament, although no reference to such a three-part God had been made during the original writings.

Perhaps there have been—and will continue to be—events and causes in our human society that make it necessary to work through agents. Most people find it convenient and less frustrating to use a real estate agent when purchasing property. My wife and I regularly rely on a travel agent when we plan long, involved trips. For a safeguard against the future, we deal with insurance agents. However, when it comes to God, it seems to me that there is no substitute for dealing directly.

For the majority of people, religion, with all of its hodgepodge, seems to be the most important factor in life. Those same people, assuming honesty prevails, would confess that their religion is, for the most part, inherited or borrowed and they do not give it serious thoughtfulness. Of course, religion comes into greater prominence for all of us in times of sickness, death, and calamity. Church attendance increases in times of financial depression, war, and other hardships in society that cause us to more seriously consider all phases of life. Perhaps, for most Americans, religion is simply a matter of social and personal convenience for the present, and a safeguard against disaster here and hereafter.

Religion is not magic. Faith is good, and, of course, faith comes through believing. But if, for any reason, we believe in the ridiculous simply because it has religious overtones, the results will be disappointing and our faith in vain. Faith is strengthened by reason.

It is comforting to assume that simply believing and confessing, which can be done in minutes, will bring answers to all of life's problems. Obviously, confession is good for the soul and forgiveness brings a new view and hope in life. However, there must be more. Future life must show a new spiritual awareness and greater appreciation for all of God's blessings. Many churches preach about the new birth (i.e., starting your spiritual life anew). However, it goes without saying that following birth, there must be nourishment, growth, and purpose.

One of the universities that I served was experiencing financial difficulties when I arrived. Among several moves calculated to bring financial stability was an attempt to collect unpaid debts for tuition, room, and board from students who had been permitted to graduate, owing the institution. As president, I sent out a letter to alumni with outstanding accounts, explaining that the payment of their bill would help us continue to educate students with the same quality programs that they had received. The plan worked rather well; a large number of alumni paid their bills in full with accompanying letters of apology for not satisfying their indebtedness at an earlier date.

I will never forget one letter that came in response to my general appeal. It was from a lady who had graduated approximately twelve years earlier and owed a rather substantial amount for unpaid tuition, room, and board. In her letter, she informed me clearly and somewhat defiantly, "God has miraculously forgiven my past and that includes my debt to the university!" After the initial shock, I chuckled about that letter many times. Some religious fervor prospers best in an atmosphere of naiveté. We all wish to be loved, and when we do wrong, we desire forgiveness. However, reason would dictate that when forgiven, we should wish to right the wrongs previously committed, if at all possible. It is undebatable that religion changes people's lives. That change is most positive when the religion, particularly when newly found, is taken with large doses of reason and common sense.

We are all part of God's creation. Along with the stars, the moon, sun, and planets, God created us. Therefore we should serve Him in an intelligent and practical manner.

As stated previously, my intent is not to be critical of any person or their religion; but I would have you, my family, and friends think seriously about what you say you believe. Make sure that it is your own and not borrowed religion. If you do, believing becomes broadening and wonderful and life becomes better day by day. For every day is "the day the Lord has made" for us to enjoy. We should live each day in such a way that is an honor to Him and His creation.

Questions and Points to Ponder

- Do you believe that it is reasonable that God's love could be purchased by gifts and sacrifices?

- How do you assume that the idea of a one-time sacrifice (i.e., Christ dying on the cross) actually came into being?

- Is it necessary to believe in the virgin birth and all of the miracles attributed to Christ in order to be a godly person?

- Does it seem logical that all of life's wrongdoings could be instantly eradicated by merely repeating a simple prayer? Are other steps needed to bring about change and attitude?

- Is there some reasonable limit to "accepting by faith"?

Chapter XIV:

In Conclusion

It has been about thirty years since the student asked, "Dr. Sago, tell me how to be a godly person; and please leave out the religious hodgepodge." I did not adequately answer her question at that time. I readily admit that I cannot, with any authority, answer it now. The longer that I consider the question, the more I am convinced that organized religion is, to a great extent, hodgepodge.

The heart of the question is, "How can we live a godly life?" Since it is impossible for us to describe God in any definitive manner, can we, in any sense, claim to be godly (i.e., like God)? Personally, I do not exclusively associate godliness with religion. Godliness suggests goodness, human kindness, and gentleness toward all of God's creation. As previously stated, it seems contradictory to suggest that we love God if we do not show love, appreciation, respect, and even protection for all of His creation.

I do not find it necessary to formally define God. He *is*. He is what I need. At the same time, God fills the needs of my neighbors, perhaps in an entirely different fashion compared to His dealings with me. For all of us, God *is*. God is the power that fuels our lives from moment to moment.

I have two grown sons. I am their father, and I love them without limit. They are both successful in their chosen fields. I am a proud father. It would be difficult for me, as their father, if my sons argued to the point of separation about which one loves me most and understands me more completely. Sometimes in my pondering, it occurs to me that God must be disappointed in His children who argue to the point of separation over who loves the Father best.

Loving God seems easy and vastly rewarding until it is mixed with the never-ending complexities of organized religion. Even the hodgepodge associated with worship becomes frustrating. Conflicting doctrines within the church become confusing. With all the hodgepodge in churchianity, it is sometimes difficult to worship God. There are many distractions: denominationalism, differing creeds and doctrines, facilities, budgets, tithing, competition within the church community, and the human tendency toward exclusiveness.

I appreciate the church. It is important for believers to unite in fellowship and purpose. However, it is even more crucial that believers understand what they believe and not permit their God to become lost in the hectic hustle of religiosity.

So, what shall we conclude? God *is*. He is for me all I permit Him to be. God provides me with limitless opportunities. Then, of course, it is my duty and responsibility to take full advantage of the opportunities presented and to do so with reason and thanksgiving. My neighbors across the street or around the world may relate to God in a different fashion. They speak to Him in a different language. They call upon Him using other names. Good for them! Why can't we learn to rejoice together?

Logical belief is a powerful force. To believe is critical to being. To know what we believe and to have our beliefs be our own, and, at the same time, to love and cooperate with others who may worship differently, brings peace and comfort that is only equaled by appreciation and praise.

I hope that we may all agree with the Old Testament prophet, Isaiah, chapter 6, verse 3: "Holy, holy, holy is the Lord of Hosts, the whole earth is full of His glory!" But the holiness of hodgepodge is, at best, an illusion. It promotes frustration and guilt, the lessening of perceived self-worth, and mental anguish for those intended to enjoy God's vast and wonderful world.

The good news is that, in spite of it all, the earth is and will continue to be full of His glory. Peace and contentment await you. God is all you need; His wonders are real; blessings for you are ready. The question is: are you ready to receive all that He intended for you?